Consiliō et Animīs

Tracing a Path to
Social Justice Through the Classics

A Volume in
Contemporary Language Education

Series Editor:
Terry Osborn, *South Florida, Sarasota-Manatee*

Contemporary Language Education

Terry Osborn, Series Editor

Consiliō et Animīs

Tracing a Path to
Social Justice Through the Classics

by

Antoinette M. Ryan
EASTCONN Regional Educational Service Center

Information Age Publishing, Inc.
Charlotte, North Carolina • www.infoagepub.com

Library of Congress Cataloging-in-Publication Data

Ryan, Antoinette Maria, 1962-
Consilio et animis : tracing a path to social justice through the classics
/ by Antoinette M. Ryan.
p. cm.
Includes bibliographical references.
ISBN 978-1-61735-883-8 (pbk.) -- ISBN 978-1-61735-884-5 (hc) --
ISBN 978-1-61735-885-2 (ebk) 1. Classical philology--Study and
teaching--United States. 2. Classical literature--Study and
teaching--United States. 3. Critical pedagogy--United States. 4. Social
justice--Study and teaching--United States. I. Title.
PA78.U6R93 2012
480.071--dc23

2012020191

Copyright © 2012 IAP–Information Age Publishing, Inc.

Printed in the United States of America

CONTENTS

PREFACE

Fifteen years ago, I attended a lecture and reading by the late Robert Fagles, whose wonderfully contemporary translations of Homer's *Iliad* and *Odyssey* and Vergil's *Aeneid* brought classical literature to the bestseller lists and bookstores, and into classrooms and homes of the twenty-first century. In a conversation following the lecture, Professor Fagles urged me to "follow my classical heart," which I did almost immediately. I promptly ended my corporate career and became a high school Latin teacher, at a time when—*mirabile dictu*—classical studies were in the midst of resurgence in secondary schools. It was as a teacher that my education truly began, and my students have been encouraging, challenging, and loving teachers. My experiences with them were the inspiration for this study, so it is to my students—past, present, and future—and to Dr. Fagles's memory, that I dedicate much of my effort herein.

This book is the product of my doctoral dissertation, completed at Central Connecticut State University. I am especially grateful to my advisor, Dr. Timothy G. Reagan, to whom I extend my deepest gratitude for his wise hand in guiding me forward in the discovery that this study represents. His unique insight continues to open new avenues for me in thought, exploration and action. I am also grateful to my dissertation committee members, Dr. Karen Beyard, Dr. Terry A. Osborn, and Dr. Mitchell Sakofs, for their excellent insights, questions, and suggestions; and, to Dr. Beyard, a special thanks for maintaining a vision for the doctoral program in Educational Leadership at Central Connecticut State University that offers transformation for those who go through it. I would also like to thank members of the New England Philosophy of Education Society (to whom I was fortunate to have presented two portions of this study) for their helpful suggestions.

Finally, to my family—my husband Tom, my children, Samantha and Jack, and my parents, Richard and Phyllis—ever my cheerleaders, my inspiration, and the loves in my life: *"possunt quia posse videntur"*—*multas gratias semper ago.*

It should be noted that all translations from Latin, Greek, French, and Portuguese into English are my own, unless otherwise noted. I have attempted to be faithful to both the meaning and the spirit of the words and the authors' expression. For those who are not fully comfortable with Latin or Greek, translations not included in the text are provided before the references.

CHAPTER 1

CONSILIUM

A Rationale for a
Critical Pedagogy of Classics

Hoc quoque nescio quid nostris appone libellis, diverso missum quod tibi ab
orbe venit. Quod quicumque leget (si quis leget) aestime ante, compositum
quo sit tempore quoque loco. Aequus erit scriptis, quorum
cognoverit esse exilium tempus barbariamque locum: inque tot adversis
carmen mirabitur ullum ducere me tristi sustinuisse manu.

—Ovid (Tristia III, xiv. 25-32)

Place also this trifle with my little books, which has come to you, sent
from a remote world. Whoever should read it (if someone reads it),
let him consider beforehand the time and place in which it has been
composed. He will be fair to the writing, when he knows that it was a
time of exile in a barbarian place: and he will be amazed that, in
such adversity I brought forth any poem, that with my sad hand I
have endured.

We who are teachers and students of classical languages[1] may find ourselves to be, like Ovid, in *exilium tempus barbariamque locum*, in a place in
which our identities might be out of sync, sometimes painfully so, with what
we encounter. We are out of place in our time, as we study the language and

Consiliō et Animīs: Tracing a Path to Social Justice Through the Classics, pp. 1–16
Copyright © 2012 by Information Age Publishing
All rights of reproduction in any form reserved.

culture of an existence far removed from our experiences; in our foreign, or "world," language departments, learning and teaching a "dead" language amid the modern, "living" language courses; in our community, because, to many, our study of Latin or Greek appears to be at best an antiquarian curiosity, or at worst, an undertaking largely irrelevant to the needs of students and society of the modern world.[2] There is only the text or the artifact that mediates the space between the modern and the ancient world; there is no place to which we can go to immerse ourselves in the "authentic" experience of a language in its cultural context. Our competence in the classical languages and cultures we attempt to understand depends on and is defined by what we create in the classroom, in private study, in museums or in visits to ancient sites together, teacher and students. We hope that, as time goes on, we can "know" something about the ancients, that we endure our explorations despite the difficult challenges of being separated by space and time, and that we are rewarded somehow for our efforts to understand them by understanding more about ourselves.

Teachers of Classics[3] share with their colleagues in modern languages many things: the difficulties of navigating through the Scylla and Charybdis of current and past discourses in language teaching and learning, such as proficiency versus mastery of language, of formal versus functional grammar, of how language is best acquired (and to what ends), and of what "culture" actually is, and how it can be studied or taught (Abbott, 1998; Álvarez, 2007; Kramsch, 2000; Krashen & Terrell, 1983; LaFleur, 1998). As are their modern language colleagues, teachers of Classics are guided in constructions of curriculum, instruction, and assessment by the "Five C's" of the *National Standards for Foreign Language Learning*: communication, culture, connections, comparisons, and communities (National Standards in Foreign Language Education Collaborative Project, 1996, 1999, 2006). As is the case with anyone working within standards, language teachers bear the weight of the consequences of their interpretations of the meanings and practical applications of the *Standards* in their teaching.

There are, therefore, crucial struggles that students and teachers of classical and modern foreign languages share. In part, these relate to the context in which foreign language education takes place in the United States. Claire Kramsch (2000) points out that "what makes foreign language study unique among the subjects taught in an academic curriculum is that its object or purpose is itself located outside the American linguistic and cultural norm" (p. 321). According to Kramsch, among the benefits of foreign language learning are the opportunities present to engage the learner in an "outsider's view," both of the realities of other academic practices and of the culture(s) within and outside of which they exist. These benefits have not created any easy partnerships among other academic disciplines, despite the fact that language teaching and learning can and does have the capacity to cast a fresh look at interdisciplinary opportunities, nor do they mitigate the impact of the flawed arguments against serious attention to foreign language learning, arguments that have plagued foreign language educators for decades, even centuries, in the United States. Reagan and Osborn (2002), in their discussion of the ideological and political constraints on foreign language education in the United States, provocatively state that "of all the academic subjects normally offered in American public schools, no other discipline is asked to defend its existence in the way that foreign language is routinely challenged" (p. 11). They further point out that, while it would seem absurd for "core" subjects of the standard high school curriculum (such as mathematics, social studies, the sciences, and English) to be optional for students just because there are those who do not view them as "applicable" to their goals for their current or future lives, foreign language educators and departments are almost constantly reminded of the fact that in difficult economic times or when resources available are limited, foreign language education in the United States is, ultimately, dispensable. Much of the discourse that has deemed foreign language education as unnecessary goes something like this: foreign language education does not serve market values particularly well, at least as it is conceived by current ideology, nor, in the U.S. setting, does it have an immediate, practical or measurable relationship to profitability or economic advantage. Foreign language education is not useful because most people will never have the opportunity, or will not need, to communicate extensively with people from other countries, and, since now most of the world speaks English anyway (as the popular wisdom goes), it may never be necessary to learn another language (Hymes, 1996; Reagan, 2002a). Arguments against the utility or relevance of classical language learning have been even more vigorous, to the extent that instruction in Latin and, especially, Greek at the secondary level threatened virtually to disappear in 1970s and 1980s (LaFleur, 1987, 1998; Watzke, 2003). After all, if there is little utility in U.S. students learning a modern foreign language, there is even far less in learning a classical one.

It seems that, so often in language education, we resist the discomfort of our relative isolation by using default modes of thinking and action: using a shield of "foreign-ness"[4] or "otherness" to describe what we are learning about or examining; accepting a standard of learning, reinforced by established ideologies and the policies they have produced, that has not alleviated the profound monolingualism of the United States that Reagan and Osborn (2002) describe; using methodologies and supporting materials in language instruction that inhibit our achievement of high levels of competence and capacity for communication, connections or cultural understandings. In classical language education, the foreign-ness of ancient languages combines with their labels as dead languages to create a distance difficult for teachers and students alike to traverse in the main-stream, particularly secondary school, environment. There is some irony in the fact that, just as Latin language and culture had exerted cultural dominance over the vast span of its *Imperium*, to the point of often sub-suming, but not necessarily eliminating, that of the "Other" (see Adams, 2003), modern proponents of the study of classical studies now struggle to maintain even a small presence in schools due to the marginalization of Classics in the twentieth and twenty-first centuries (despite a resurgence of Latin in public schools; see LaFleur, 1998). More insidiously, as educa-tion in Latin and Greek in the past served not a small role in establishing and maintaining power and cultural hegemony in the West, the renewed call for classical education in recent years has come in part from cultural and political conservatives in the United States, who advocate a return to the Classics in education as a means of recalling and strengthening "tradi-tional" time-honored wisdom, "family values," and as a basis for advanc-ing a neoconservative political agenda fortified by the use of Platonic philosophy and ideas (Bennett, 1993; Hanson & Heath, 1998; Kopff, 2000; also, see Robertson, 2006, on Leo Strauss and the neoconserva-tives). There are those in Classics who have countered the conservative agenda regarding Classics by instead focusing on the opportunities that the study of classical cultures presents as a resource for critical analyses of contemporary politics and societies. One of the most notable and succinct expressions of this viewpoint comes from Page duBois, whose book, *Trojan Horses: Saving the Classics From Conservatives* (2001), provides an eloquent rationale for studying Classics from a critical standpoint:

> Ancient Greek society is *one* of the sources of contemporary culture, emi-nently worthy of being known and understood as such.... But even more, the Greeks are fascinating because they were not like us, because, although we owe to them some of the institutions through which we organize our own culture, they did it all quite differently, and therefore offer us difference from ourselves, other voices.... Let us, in the inexhaustible study of Greek antiquity, recover unfamiliar traces of the ancient past. (p. 137)

Longa tibi exilium

In those remote spaces that are so often the province of language edu-cation, the unexpected happens:

> *Dicere saepe aliquid conanti (turpe fateri) verba mihi desunt dedidicique loqui. Threicio Scythicoque fere circumsonor ore, et videor Geticis scribere posse modis.*
>
> —Ovid (Tristia, III, xiv. 45-49)

In trying to say something (I shamefully confess) words leave me
and I forget how to speak. I am nearly surrounded by the sound of
Thracian and Scythian mouths, and I seem to be able to write in
Getic modes.

Ovid's reaction to exile in Tomis, on the Black Sea, in a place considered by the Romans to be the furthest outpost of the *Imperium*, reveals
both an unflattering view of the Roman cosmopolitan and also a notion of
"punishment" that is illustrative of one aspect of Roman ideas concerning
"foreignness." For a Roman aristocrat to be forced to inhabit a wild, "un-
Romanized" place, isolated from language and culture, appears to have
been a dire consequence indeed.[5] Finding himself forgetting words in his
native Latin as he begins to internalize the words and manners of speech
of his "barbarian" hosts, Ovid has an experience that those who study languages may also come to know, one that pokes holes into preconceived
identities, once-solid assumptions of thought, of ways of being and knowing, of constructions of Self and Other that break down. Face-to-face with
the unknown, doors open that lead us to ask critical questions. Those
questions bear fruits of new understandings, and as educators who accom-
pany students on a journey to learn about worlds we can never actually
traverse, we have the unique responsibility to reflect with them upon what
they may view as true or given, and on what they may not understand,
given the paradigms within which they currently operate. Michael Apple
(2004) describes the endeavor of the educator who confronts her/himself
on such questions:

> One must bracket any commitment to the utility of employing our taken for
> granted perspectives so that these commonsense presuppositions can
> become subject to investigation ..., used as *data* to focus upon the latent sig-
> nificance of much that we unquestioningly do in schools. (p. 119, emphasis
> in original)

The "outsider's view," referred to by Kramsch above, has the potential
and potency of a critical stance, one that questions the presuppositions in
current discourses that have created and have been created by the intents,
purposes, and methods in teaching languages. Between the insider's view
of practice and the outsider's view of possibility, there is a new place
afforded the teacher of classical languages and culture, and it is this place
that this dissertation explores.

In an effort to confront some presuppositions about teaching Classics
in the twenty-first century (in particular, some frequently-asserted
assumptions regarding its relevance for modern concerns, and the utility
of a "dead" language), this study proposes a critical approach to and
rationale for incorporating the study of Classics in American public

schools. I argue for a renewed vision for secondary education in classical (specifically, Latin and Greek) languages, culture and history that is grounded in a critical pedagogical stance. This argument proceeds from the position that the study of Classics provides students with a uniquely wide range of opportunities for critical examination of the impact of language, cultural constructions of power, knowledge, and oppression in society. It considers the capacity of foreign language pedagogy to perpetuate or remediate dynamics and imbalances of power in society, and evaluates pedagogy in classical studies in this regard. The key concern here is that, in order for Classics to enhance the critical potential in the education of students in the United States, its purposes, standards and processes must provide opportunities for students to become critically curious, reflective and action oriented as they explore the interplay of language learning, culture and the broad concerns of social justice. Michel Foucault's (1969, 1969/1972, 1980, 2000, 2007) descriptions of the relationships among power and knowledge, discourse and truth, are a connecting thread among all of the issues considered here, and are vitally important to uncovering a history of Classics' past and present in education in the United States, which is the focus of Chapter 2. Chapter 3 is a discussion of critical pedagogy as it has emerged in the United States, from its initial impulses in the mid-1800s to the evolution in critical theory in the first half of the twentieth century, to the incorporation of Paulo Freire's notion of praxis, and its present state in education in general and in foreign language education in particular. In Chapter 4, the national standards for foreign language and classical language learning are reviewed, with a focus on bringing the "critical" into the evaluation, particularly as that notion is informed by current questions being raised by issues in critical pedagogy, critical language studies and second-language acquisition. In Chapter 5, I seek to connect the strands that emerge from each of the previous chapters and weave them into an exploration of areas in which teachers of Classics may engage with their students in critical reflection on their world that can lead to action for social justice. In the end, this study seeks to broaden perspectives on the potential for and impact of critical engagement in teaching and learning in Classics, for, as Foucault so aptly stated, "People know what they do; they frequently know why they do what they do; but what they don't know is what what they do does" (Foucault, as cited in Dreyfus & Rabinow, 1983, p. 187).

Decipimur specie recti

As the twenty-first century began to dawn on the American political horizon, calls for education reform [from the *alarum* sounded by *A Nation at Risk* (Gardner, 1983) to the truly alarming No Child Left Behind Act of 2002] forced a contentious and often politically partisan debate on the persistent question of what to do and how to do it in education. Proceeding from an emphasis on the economic value of education that has undergirded public schooling since the middle of the nineteenth century (Mulcahy, 2008; Tozer, Violas, & Senese, 2002), the espoused aims of education for individual success and national competitiveness in social, economic and global arenas have created a system that has embraced corporate language related to productivity and market competition, and has nearly silenced the voices that would offer challenges to its hegemonic practices and realities (Giroux, 2005). The current discourses in education surrounding "reform" and "accountability" operate from notions of deficiency: that students and educators are deficient; that parents' and communities' commitments to educational forms and systems are deficient; that in most respects the human element is deficient and needs to be "fixed." Stephen Ball (1990, 2001) provides a useful perspective for understanding such evaluations. Extending Foucault's description of the discourses deployed by institutions in society in practices that serve to classify, control and contain individuals and groups [what Ball refers to as "dividing practices" (1990, p. 4)], he refers to "performativity," a system that controls through judgment, comparisons and measurements of performances of individuals, subjects, and organizations (see also Pennycook, 2004b). The discourses of performativity include "accountability," and "competition" or "competitiveness" as justification for what passes as "reform" in education in our society. How the concept of "the educated person" (see Dearden, Hirst, & Peters, 2004; Hirst, 2010, Hirst & Peters, 1970; Martin, 2002, Mulcahy, 2008) has changed over the years is part of the effect of performativity. When it comes to evaluation in education, Ball points out, it is no longer the organization of power or what is actually done that is important, but rather, it is the means of judging and the fact of being judged, a constant flow of accountability, that is emphasized. This has created what Ball (2001, 2003) refers to as ontological insecurity —instability, uncertainty, guilt and fear that what is done is not "good enough." Performativity impacts what is done, what is created and what motivates which types of action, and thrives when educational principles and policies are bound to national economic competitiveness (Ball, 2001, p. 212). In this insecure state, to make matters more dangerous in a Foucauldian sense, success and productivity is measured against an ambiguous or amorphous global market, and in terms of a so-called global competition for which our students must be prepared (see Friedman, 2006). Additionally, there are the pervasive assumptions regarding the benefits of standardization in education: that standards should or can in fact be set for what students should learn, that standardization of curricula can provide guarantees for what students learn, that the articulated standards are appropriate and valid for what all students need to know, and that such learning can be adequately or appropriately measured through standardized tests (see Ravitch, 1995[6]). Another such perspective is that certain curricula, knowledge and skills have inherent relevance, utility and value to the market, and that the connection to "the market" should drive the goals of education (Beyer & Apple, 1998; Teitelbaum, 1998). In all of the rhetoric surrounding the use of standards to assure "achievement," achievement equals competitiveness. Never, in the calculus of standards-based education or assessment of achievement, is there the mention of other, perhaps "softer," though no less challenging goals and values, such as humanitarianism, compassion, empathy and understanding, or social justice.

To the extent that the rules of relevance, utility, market value and competition remain embedded in the collective beliefs about the purposes of education in our society, education in Classics, like liberal arts education, will continue to have its detractors and struggle to maintain its place, even at the margins of curriculum. Yet, this dissertation argues that Classics offers a form of resistance to such dangerous "truth games" (see Ball, 1990, essentially a Foucauldian warning) that are being played out in today's educational arenas. To be sure, classical education established and was established by hegemonic practices in the Western educational tradition (Gramsci & Buttigieg, 2002; Janson, 2004; Waquet, 2001), and it is important to acknowledge that, in many respects, the direction that education in the United States took in the nineteenth century was a form of resistance to the hegemony of Classics (Meckler, 2006, Pearcy, 2005; Winterer, 2002). While knowledge of classical languages and literature once was the hallmark of an excellent educational pedigree, the discourses promoting anti-elitism and "purposeful" education grew more strident as the twentieth century approached. Classical education in the United States became increasingly marginalized by educational priorities deemed more expedient to creating productive members of an American workforce. Ideologies in language education, which began to focus on criteria related to practicality and utility, deemed certain modern European languages more practical than classical languages; these ideologies continue to dictate the viability of certain languages in school curricula (Watzke, 2003). In the twentieth and twenty-first centuries, the United States government's policies have also played a key role in asserting the importance of language education, in the context of education reform and a broader national agenda. The establishment of the so-called "mission critical languages" category that the U.S. government has deemed essential for the country's defense system[7] indicates that the value inherent in language learning has more to do, ultimately, with protection and profit of American interests than for what it may have to offer to bring United States citizens into an integrated, interculturally-literate relationship with the world.

Quo usque tandem abutere...?

Tracing the evolution of the purposes of education and of the concept of the "educated person," particularly through the twentieth and twenty-first centuries, is important to understanding the role that classical and modern language education has played, and continues to play, in the United States. An historic perspective may further illuminate the dilemmas faced by generations of teachers and students of languages, dilemmas surrounding what is or has been important in language study, what constitutes "competence" or which "competencies" can be taught effectively, and which ones matter in the lives of individuals and in the collective, public sphere. Ultimately, the context within which these issues arose and the discourses established by them cannot be separated from the effects they have had on the culture they have created. To a significant extent, the ideals in foreign language education share with "education," writ large, a context that is inseparable from those concepts. As Reagan (2009b) has argued, "what constitutes an 'educated person' is necessarily tied to time and place, and [there] really cannot be any 'neutral' conception of either 'education' or the 'educated person'" (p. 5).

Jane Roland Martin's (2002) excellent discussion regarding the effects of "cultural miseducation" (see also Chomsky & Macedo, 2000) is instructive regarding what is missing in the conversation about what matters in education. Acknowledging the fact that cultures transmit "liabilities" from one generation to the next is an essential step toward assuming a critical stance in education. According to Martin, one of the aspects of the miseducation we have engaged in is the idea that educational reform begins from perspective of the individual. That is, because the focus in the evaluation of educational institutions and systems has largely been on individual successes and failures, or the successes and failures of certain identified groups in society, we have missed (or avoided) a broader examination of the cultural influences on, and of, education. As Martin asserts, the focus on the individual is, and has always been, problematic, given the number of questions it raises. Who is this "educated person" whom so many educational theorists and philosophers have written about and idealized? What or whom does this person represent? Should we be concerned that this discourse was originally based on the idea that education was primarily and very narrowly focused on the White male destined to take his place in society to assume a role that his experiences had shaped for him? The biggest problem, according to Martin, is that while we are focused on the education of a child or of children, our attention is diverted from the number and variety of educational phenomena that create the education that transmits culture. Not only schools, but churches, communities, cultural and public institutions of all sorts create the cultural wealth that is part of the creation of an education, an education that underpins not only individual experiences and capacities and potential, but those of the society as a whole. While it is not the intention of this study to explore the impact of culture's educational agents in the manner of Martin, it is relevant to consider the place that Humanities and Classics has occupied, particularly in the twentieth and twenty-first centuries, and the educational agents that have delivered ideas about such disciplines.

Traditionally, disciplines in humanities held the responsibility for perpetuating the "cultural wealth" that Americans had attached themselves to in their relatively brief educational history. Classics, once the core of the humanities, has had a long and checkered history since the beginnings of public secondary and higher education in the United States. Perhaps because of its connection to European models of education, perhaps because of the lessons that ancient Greek and Roman culture represented to the Founders, the elements of classical learning (primarily language, culture, history, mythology) have been considered throughout the history of education in America alternately as essential, as anachronistic, as liberating, as hegemonic (Pearcy, 2005; Winterer, 2002). Classical literature and history have been hijacked in recent years by the most conservative elements, the result of which has been that many of the ideas and much of the intention behind those ideas have been reinterpreted, revised and reinvented to suit political, rather than educational, purposes (see duBois, 2001, for commentary on this). Therefore, it is wise to approach cautiously the use of what have become rather loaded terms (e.g., those having to do with Western traditions, virtues, and ideals) in discussions regarding the value of Classics and humanities in retaining the cultural wealth of our society. Mulcahy (2008) describes a "distinct utilitarian streak" that has characterized modern American education, one that has countered the humanistic ideal that had existed previously. He argues that the "ambiguity" in perceptions about the purpose of education gave way to a "marketplace of noises" that, although initially discordant, ultimately found their focus in the rhetoric of "excellence" and "competitiveness" in the late 1950s (pp. 8-9). The association with humanities and classical studies with higher education, either as a hallmark of higher education or as a path to entering higher education, has in part been responsible for their lack of significant presence in elementary and secondary schools that have operated as institutions that feed the workplace.

However, in recent years the concerns about the substance of education in the United States have turned a hackneyed outcry—that our children do not know how to think, creatively, independently, or logically—into a criticism that sounds almost novel: that as humanities education has taken a back seat to emphases on more practical (widely regarded as math- and science-related) education, so too has students' ability to think. In a recent article, journalist Mark Slouka (2009) issued a scathing indictment of the business community's impact on education, the blind acceptance by the public of its influence, and the government and policymakers' agreement that what is good for business is good for education. He asserts that the American "love affair" with math and science as the panacea for the ailing economy and for the loss of ground in a global marketplace, in which Asia appears to be edging out the West in terms of profit and productivity, has had dramatic and deleterious effects on the quality of education at the elementary, secondary, and higher education levels, as education in Humanities and arts has been rather devalued.

Slouka (2009) is not alone in his dismay. There have been many who have expressed concerns that, in the drive toward standardized curricula (e.g. see Mathis, 2010) and assessments focused on discrete skills in math, science and reading, educational policy in the United States is leaving behind "liberal education," a foundation of the Western educational tradition. As Mulcahy (2008), Reagan (2009b) and others (Hirst, 2010; Shor, 1992) have pointed out, what constitutes "liberal education" is neither unproblematic nor easily defined. However, the study of language, literature, philosophies and histories—traditionally the province of humanities—has been viewed as central to the development of the ability to create, to think critically, to communicate meaningfully, and to understand the essence of becoming "fully human" (see Kronman, 2007). In this regard, the study of languages is central, as Elgin (2000) describes:

> We forget, or are unaware of, the power that language has over our minds and our lives.... We make major decisions about language on the most flimsy and trivial—and often entirely mistaken—grounds. (p. 239)

As Reagan (2009b) and Kronman (2008) remind us, the value of a liberal education is that, in exploring a variety of disciplines, we also learn to understand the world through different lenses, through the problems they pose about the world, and in the way that the thinking behind those disciplines creates an organization of the world for us to consider. The ability to view the world through a variety of lenses is the starting point for a critical education, and the foundation for the pursuit of teaching and learning for social justice.

Martin's (2002) perspective on cultural wealth is relevant to an examination of the role of Classics as a route to critical education because it can help illuminate the contribution that classical education has made to the cultural legacy, and liability, in the United States. It may be appropriate to begin with some of the liabilities associated with classical education. Its legacy as a tool for teaching the cultural and political elite cannot be easily dismissed in a defense of classical education, and it has, at the very least, led to an image problem, in a way, that those who teach and learn Classics have struggled with mightily, especially in recent decades. Paul Cartledge (1998) explores the role of Classics and classical education as a battering ram in the brand of "culture wars" that has taken place in the United States and in England, in which the battle rages over what makes for important, relevant and "core" education. Classics, he says, has been politicized in a "pronounced fetishizing of culture as a religion-substitute, a sort of fundamentalism by other means" (p. 17). Indeed, there has been much extolling of the virtues and messages that the Classics and classical tradition have to "teach" modern society, in media and in books and articles written by classicists meant for both a scholarly and a populist reading in the United States (e.g., see Hanson & Heath, 1998; Kopff, 2000). Popular perception of classical learning appears to be rather pointedly skewed toward the conservative aspects of a pedagogy that served generations of students from the cultural and intellectual elite, and to the relative mismatch that the "deadness" of ancient Greek and Latin is to a twenty-first century education.

Yet, we may put aside, if only temporarily, the arguments about the value of "Great Books" or the oppressive "tradition" of the Classics, and whom or what they represent, about why and how students should learn Classics and classical languages (especially when the arguments deteriorate into territorial rifts). It is also possible to see Classics through a lens such as one that Antonio Gramsci (2002) suggested, as noted in Apple, Au and Gandin (2009b), that "the tasks of a truly counter-hegemonic practice in education is not to throw out 'élite knowledge' but to reconstruct its form and content so that it served genuinely progressive social needs" (p. 4, note 4). Given the place in education that Classics occupied for centuries as one such source of élite knowledge, there is also great potential for Classics to be reconstructed to empower and emancipate, particularly through the philosophical questions that have been pondered in classical cultures (and in classical studies) since antiquity. Some essential social, political and ethical questions of 2000 B.C.E. are, at their core, the same questions of 2000 C.E. (noted by Beard & Henderson, 2000; Reagan, 2009a). The questions that are eternally ours, eternally centered in the human condition, are the province of Classics. Yet we must also avoid a facile patterning of our modern cultural understandings and perceptions along ancient Greek and Roman lines. Rather, the great value in pursuing knowledge of Classics and classical culture exists in what we discover about the nature of differences among modern and ancient approaches to those questions, and, as duBois (2001) writes, in the "manifold, various, often contradictory and ambiguous repertory, a lost compendium of human practices" (p. 136).

The issues that concern the "criticals"—such as critical theory, critical pedagogy, and critical applied linguistics—have long held an important place in classical thought. The "critical" that is explored in this study is the critical that has been very broadly and rather ambiguously defined in modern philosophy and by those theorists who have contributed to the development of ideas in critical pedagogy and critical applied linguistics. Critical theory, whose origins have been generally associated with the philosophers and theorists of the Frankfurt School, has often been associated with Marxist and post-Marxist thought. While the nature of critical theory and critical pedagogy will be reviewed in Chapter 3, it is important to note here the issues at the heart of critical theory that lend themselves to the discussion of the relevance that Classics has as in modern education. Plato and Aristotle, Homer and Sophocles, Cicero and Vergil each contemplated matters of justice and injustice, ethics and inhumanity, power and the corruptive force of power. Despite conveniently conservative notions about the messages that classical literature has to offer, those who teach and learn Classics have a unique and broad range of opportunities to explore the connections among truth, power and knowledge, and between power and resistance. The Greeks and Romans struggled as we struggle now. It is difficult to imagine an issue that the world faces today that was not part of the ancient world, and we have a fortune of ancient ponderings about such issues close at hand in classical studies. Rather than looking to the classical tradition for answers, we may reflect on classical history, literature and art, as entry points for critical questions. Beard and Henderson (2000) frame the nature of modern interactions with the Classics in this way, which provides a fitting transition to the remainder of this study:

> *Classics* is a subject that exists in that gap between us and the world of the Greeks and Romans. The questions raised by *Classics* are the questions raised by our distance from "their" world, and at the same time by our closeness to it, and by its familiarity to us.... The aim of *Classics* is not only to *discover* or *uncover* the ancient world.... Its aim is also to define and debate our relationship to that world. (pp. 6-7, emphases in original)

Further, Beard and Henderson (2000) state, "If *Classics* exists ... in the 'gap' between our world and the ancient world, then *Classics* is defined by our experiences, interests and debates as well as by theirs" (pp. 34-35, emphases in original). Those experiences are what the study of Classics offers very broadly, yet with the potential for razor-sharp focus, to modern students, who must have the opportunity ask critical questions, to question assumptions about the way things are, and who shoulder the burden of change and chaos, constants in a world in which humanity seeks an illusion of control through understanding. For American students, particularly in secondary schools, classical studies offer a grounding for a dialogue of the "negotiable self," an opportunity for engagement in what Pearcy (2005) calls "an intellectual praxis" in which we may consider our systems of thought in action, the ways in which we "negotiate" culture, toward a more socially-conscious, and, ultimately, socially responsible way of being in the world. For all of the discourse surrounding competition, training, and the relative importance of curricula, Classics' greatest gift for American students may be in the light it sheds on the path of social justice.

NOTES

1.   Throughout this dissertation, the term "classical languages" will refer specifically to ancient Greek and Latin. I must acknowledge that this is an extremely Eurocentric choice, however, as there are classical languages that have had worldwide influence and importance, such as Sanskrit, Tamil, Arabic, Aramaic, Classical Chinese, Hebrew, and so on. George Hart (2000), professor of Tamil at the University of California, Berkeley, offered a reasonable definition of classical languages: "To qualify as a classical tradition, a language must fit several criteria: it should be ancient, it should be an independent tradition that arose mostly on its own not as an offshoot of another tradition, and it must have a large and extremely rich body of ancient literature" (p. 1). There are perhaps equally reasonable arguments against portions (or perhaps all of) this statement (particularly the requirement of a "body of ancient literature," which results in a de facto exclusion of many valuable aspects of ancient languages, including Greek and Latin language, for example, of nonliterary Latin and Latin language variants, and cross-language communications), but for the purposes of this study, it at least in part explains the designation of ancient Greek and Latin as classical languages. Further, the use of the term "classical" in reference exclusively to ancient Greek and Latin is essentially a convenient convention, in use in Western education for centuries, and still in use. For further discussion, see also note 3 below.
2.   Yun Lee Too and Niall Livingstone (1998) recount their experiences of various responses to their telling people that they are classicists, ranging from mild surprise to pats on the back to, in the case of one of the editors, expressions of dismay that she chose not to "do her own languages." As Too and Livingstone indicate, these reactions bring forth questions of for

whom classical learning is acceptable, expected or appropriate, and what its value is in terms of the power it conveys.

3. Although the term "Classics" is problematic, for reasons noted in note 1, above, Western academics still refer to Classics in general as the branch of studies that explores the ancient (especially, though not exclusively, the Mediterranean) world in its entirety. Because my personal experience in Classics has included the traditional Western interdisciplinary study of ancient Greece and Rome, including Latin and ancient Greek languages, literature, history, and cultures, it is primarily from this perspective that I approach "Classics," "classical studies," and "classical languages. As noted by Beard and Henderson (2000), the "Classics" that this study refers to is the place where our modern Western culture intersects with that portion of the ancient world to which we are very much connected, at least in language, ideology, practices and perspectives.

4. Reagan and Osborn (2002) discuss the components of "foreignness" to an extent that will not be addressed in this dissertation. However, it is instructive to acknowledge their assertion that the impact of the idea of the foreignness of non-English languages not only marginalizes the languages themselves, but also the efforts to teach them (p. 87).

5. On the other hand, it is important to note that there were other attitudes during the late-Republic and early-Empire periods regarding cultural identities. Andrew Wallace-Hadrill (2008) has written compellingly about Roman linguistic and cultural relationships with the Other ("Other" including Hellenic, Italic, and other provincial cultures) that created new constructs of knowledge and power, constructs that did not necessarily include only the patrician elite's access to power, but also saw the non-elite achieve what Wallace-Hadrill refers to as "cultural ambidexterity" (p. 5) or "cultural triangulation" among Roman, Greek and "barbarian' cultures that were a feature of the Roman world. Hadrill cites a famous quotation by Aulus Gellius in which Ennius (a B.C.E. second century writer of an epic history of Rome) talked of having "three hearts" (tria cordia), because he could speak Greek, Latin and Oscan, to describe this triangulated notion of personal identity that was a feature of Roman culture.

6. See also Ravitch's (2010) recent indictment of some of the ramifications of the standards-based education she formerly supported (Ravitch, 1995)—specifically, high-stakes testing and market-sponsored school choice. Despite her disillusionment with these aspects of a system she was in no small part responsible for initiating during the George H. W. Bush administration, she still advocates a national curriculum, with standards for what every student should learn. She has not problematized the aspects of standards-based education, as have others (Giroux, 2005; Kanpol, 1999; Popham, 2004).

7. According to a report issued by the U.S. Department of Education, Office of Post Secondary Education (2008), the National Security Language Initiative was established by the Federal Government in 2006 for the purpose of "promoting understanding, conveying respect for other cultures, and encouraging reform" in "critical world regions." The report is introduced

with a quote from former President George W. Bush: "Learning a language—somebody else's language—is a kind gesture. It is a gesture of interest. It really is a fundamental way to reach out to somebody and say, I care about you. I want you to know that I'm interested not only in how you talk but also in how you live." "Kind gestures" aside, the report further states that learning these "mission critical languages" is "fundamental to the economic competitiveness and security interests of the nation" (p. 1).

CHAPTER 2

AUCTORITAS

The Culturism of Classics in America, 1700 to the Present

> *ne vetus indigenas nomen mutare Latinos*
> *neu Troas fieri iubeas Teucrosque vocari*
> *aut vocem mutare viros aut vertere vestem.*
> *sit Latium, sint Albani per saecula reges,*
> *sit Romana potens Itala virtute propago:*
> *occidit, occideritque sinas cum nomine Troia.*
> —Vergil (Aeneid XII. 831-835)

> May you not order the native Latins to change their ancient name,
> nor to become Trojans or to be called Teucrians, or that the men
> change their language or modify their dress. Let Latium be, may the
> Albans be kings throughout the ages, may Roman power be bred
> with Italian courage; Troy fell; may you allow that it will have fallen
> with its name.

In Juno's plea to Jupiter near the end of the Roman epic *Aeneid*, that the name, the dress and the language of the Latins be preserved for all time, the poet Vergil gives voice to what he took to be the sacred in his own culture. Those *signa* that the Latins held dear, elements that shaped their individual and collective identities, would not be among the spoils of war.

Consiliō et Animis: Tracing a Path to Social Justice Through the Classics, pp. 17–42
Copyright © 2012 by Information Age Publishing
All rights of reproduction in any form reserved.

Instead, Aeneas, the leader destined to found the Roman race, would concede his Trojan heritage (and even his son's original Trojan name) to a new, more powerful, divinely-ordained amalgamation of cultures that would become Roman. For Vergil's contemporaries who bore witness to these words (primarily members of imperial Rome's élite), a remembrance of a unique, primal *gens*, the idea of a cultural essence carried in their words, clothing and name, had a deep resonance, particularly in the wake of the collapse of the Republic after nearly a century of civil war and corruption, a cultural nightmare from which Rome had just begun to emerge under Augustus' principate.[1]

It is does not require a tremendous leap to imagine the Revolutionary leaders of North America, steeped in Roman literature from their grammar-school years, envisioning a similar version of the American cultural emergence—phoenix-like, born from the flames of revolution and drawn from a heritage which they could trace back directly to Rome and Greece. As Richard (1994) states, "the Classics filled [the Founders'] days and nights, providing comfort for the distressed, adventure for the bored, and lessons, both moral and political, for the student of life" (p. 32). In his extensive study of the influence of classical literature on early American consciousness, John Shields (2001) described Revolutionary-era America as a "a time when Adam became Aeneas" (p. 75), when the Puritan emphasis on the Christian model of virtue (the Adamic mythos) gave way to a secular notion of morality embodied in the classical figure of Aeneas.[2] While there were those among the founding fathers—Benjamin Rush and Benjamin Franklin among them—(see Pearcy, 2005; and Winterer, 2002)[3] who argued that study of Classics was at best a tedious exercise, and at worst a purposeless endeavor that diverted energy from more relevant courses of study, classical education was part of the conditioning of the young American élite on their way to becoming "educated," and the tradition of classical study persisted strongly through the nineteenth century. As Henry Adams (1918) wrote (with not a small amount of cynicism), "the American boy of 1854 stood nearer the year 1 than to the year 1900" (p. 53).

This chapter provides an overview of the study and role of the Classics in America, using the work of Michel Foucault as a framework for investigating discourses—and the network of power, knowledge and truth they create—that constructed the role of classical learning during the eighteenth through twenty-first centuries. The period of the late-eighteenth century provides a starting point for this analysis, as it was during the post-Revolutionary period that education in Classics began to take on a distinctly American patina, although it is important to refer occasionally to the 100-year tradition of Classics in America that precedes it. Recent studies of classicism and classical education in America (Pearcy, 2005;

Richard, 1994, 2009; Shields, 2001; Winterer, 2002, 2006) have provided important historical background for use in this analysis. In addition, several books and papers written at the end of the nineteenth and the beginning of the early twentieth century regarding classical education in American (e.g., see Shorey, 1919; Trumbull, 1869) offer insight into the discourse regarding Classics during the period that established the modern age.

The "culturism of Classics," to which the title of this study refers,[4] is used in this chapter to employ Foucault's notion of discourse in describing Classics' effect on the American world. "Culturism" is envisioned as the systems of thought in action (following Foucault's description of power) that underpin the development and enculturation of the American ruling class, which emerged surrounded by American interpretations of classical literature, culture and language. It addresses the dominance of classical ideas and the efficacy of classical education in shaping concepts of "America" and "the American." Similarly, John Shields (2001) adopts the term *translatio cultus*, variously understood as a transfer, or transplanting, of modes of being, of educating, or of enculturating, to explain the cultural "redefinition" and "American-ness" with which classicism became imbued, as Old World "cultural imperatives" were transplanted within the New World, as evinced in the dual influences of Christianity and classical models (pp. 3-4). But the "culturism" of Classics, as it is used here, also reflects American ambivalence toward classical education, where, historically, knowledge of the Classics has been a hallmark of the "educated person" at the same time that it has been variously disconnected from or used by (primarily as references in popular culture) the general public.

Recent work by Lee T. Pearcy (2005) explores the historic purposes, presence, outcomes and future of classical education in America. Pearcy captures the idea of classical education as a structure that could "explain, encode and enact what it means to be fully human in America" (p. 120), as a form of education, rather than as an academic discipline. He asserts that, as education in general is "the grammar of a language called culture," classical education became the "enabling code, [the] grammar of civility" for the governing class in America from its early existence in the new nation until the First World War (pp. 4-5). Pearcy traces the history of classical studies into the twentieth and twenty-first centuries, during which time the presence of Classics in education has become increasingly diminished, owing to the fact that "classical studies had never become naturalized in America," and that it had been marginalized even in the liberal arts that it gave birth to in Europe and America (p. 82). Despite a relative degree of marginalization, classical studies are still grounded in an exploration of human culture (p. 133). Despite a tenuous hold on its place in secondary school curricula, Classics retains its presence in American education.

Despite its image problem as an anachronistic, stodgy, élitist, or merely difficult course of study, Classics remains most powerfully as a dialogue, as Pearcy states, "a continuous invitation to renegotiate the self against culture" (p. 132).

Pearcy's description of classical education as the structure and language that could encode values, and Shields' notion of early American *translatio cultus*, recall the concepts of "discursive formations" of "truth-objects" put forth in the work of Michel Foucault. Foucault provides a conceptual framework within which to discuss the interdependence of thoughts, words and acts that create and are created by systems in various historical points in American society. According to Foucault, in order to understand the way things are in a given point in time, the most important areas to excavate in historical analyses are the points at which elements, relationships and rules in systems change, are transformed (Foucault, 1969, 1969/1972). It is important to understand those divergences because they reveal the power of discourse to influence knowledge and for what is considered knowledge to produce systems of power. Foucault's conceptualization of "archeology" suggests that, to begin to understand these historical divisions in the history of Classics in America, we examine the statements made during particular eras that create the discourses unique to these periods, discourses that are the source that establishes what is possible to think and say.

Foucauldian analysis also offers a path for understanding the ways in which classical education has been interpreted, used, and recreated in American educational practices. Viewed from a distance, it appears that *idea* of Classics became somehow distinct from the content itself (classical languages, cultures, history, and literature) at various time periods in American history. Some classical ideals have reverberated in, and have created, a part of the American psyche. For example, the explicit and implicit call to the ideal that the Romans referred to as *pietas*—often defined as devotion to country, to duty, abandoning all personal concerns (which had its fullest expression in Roman culture in the figure of Aeneas) —has echoed in American expressions from patriotism to political propaganda, from the Founders' documents to modern-day media screed.[5] To various degrees, classical concepts and models have been alternately exploited and extolled in manifestations of educational policy and practices throughout American history; such discontinuities in discourse frame the use and disuse of Classics in American education. The concept of Classics and classical studies can be considered an object of discourse, in Foucauldian terms, in which practices of power, resistance, agency and control that are specific to the discourse of time periods create the nature of its function in and impact upon society.

Foucault's concept of "power/knowledge," and the discourses that create and function within the dynamic interaction of power and knowledge, provides a path for excavating what has been and what is now, and how discourses can be differentiated by historical period. For example, like "culturism," the concept of *auctoritas* offers another facet of the Foucauldian relationship between the enactment of power and the creation of knowledge. The ancient perspective on *auctoritas* is generally understood as political or social clout, prestige, and the capacity of an *auctor* to effect or complete some act, some legislation (Smith, 1890, p. 247). According to Galinsky (1998), auctoritas is the capacity to make things happen through an authority that is, in effect, granted by social interactions. As such, it is fluid, not a constant or guarantee that comes by virtue of one's social class or political position, but is subject to reaffirmation (or de facto denial) by those who would be ruled. Philosopher Hannah Arendt (1977) extended a vision of auctoritas that is appropriate to the foundational aspect of Classics in America: the authority borne of foundational act, and responsibilities of the Founders for the augmentation or enhancement of that foundation, and for the world they create (pp. 121-122).

Auctoritas and its particular brand of power can be analyzed using Foucault's concept of power, as can the role of the *auctor* (i.e., one possessing *auctoritas*), which can be conceived of as both one who creates and is created by power/knowledge structures. Foucault's concept of power does not exist as some entity outside of the subjects it creates; it exists only in relation to those subjects, which generate knowledges that enact power. The interrelationships of power, knowledge and subjects ultimately result in truths that are embraced by a certain present. In a history of the discourse, or "grammar" (to employ Pearcy's metaphorical use of the term), of classical education, one can trace the changes in concepts of auctoritas through various time periods, of those who possessed it, of those who enacted it (as an *auctor*) as social agents (extending the use of the etymological connection to *auctoritas*), and of those who perpetuated (or resisted) its power. An archeology of power in the United States is, in a practical sense, a history of *auctoritas*. Power created *auctoritas*; *auctoritas* created the capacity for power, and, for most of the nearly four centuries of America's existence, a classical education contributed to the creation of individuals with *auctoritas*.

As American society's self-concept changed or evolved, education, as a Foucauldian "disciplinary" structure, also changed. Foucault examined the ways in which certain institutions (such as the penal system, psychiatry, and medicine, which had been primary foci in his research and writings) were formed by power/knowledge structures as a means of regulating established norms of behavior and activities of subjects, of punishing divergences, and of observation of subjects as a means for power to maintain itself, and also for resistance to power to occur (see Foucault, 1980, 2000, 1963/2003, 1961/2006). Foucault argued that, "Every education system is a political means of maintaining or modifying the appropriateness of discourses with the knowledge and power they bring with them" (as cited in Popkewitz & Brennan, 1998, p. xiii). With the changes that occurred in structures of power in American society came modifications in the discourse of classical education, particularly in terms of its purposes, goals and pedagogical practices.

For over three centuries, students in the United States have studied classical languages and civilization in various forms and designs that have paralleled the winding course of public education (Pearcy, 2005; Winterer, 2002). The view of America that the Founders had from their classical porticos is not the same one that successive generations had as they gazed upon the physical and social world which grew up around them from those classical foundations. Though classical models were intrinsic to the architectural and political forms and ideas that emerged in Revolutionary America (Pearcy, 2005; Richard, 1994), the American experience of the world in subsequent eras was a built by "monuments" (in Foucault's [1969/ 1972] sense of the word, to describe discourses) constructed in each era by the language and gestures, assumptions and expectations, interpretations and conceptions that were made possible because of these dynamic inter-actions.

While classical foundations are apparent within the construction of these monuments, it is also important to discover the points at which the structures change, as what became possible to think diverged and some-thing new happened to those classical constructs. Foucault (1969/1972) suggests that the division between truth and falseness is "a historically constituted division," and as such, we must keep in mind that "the will to truth, like other systems of exclusion, relies on institutional support" (p. 219). Such an examination permits a critical view of classical education throughout the centuries in American culture, if we follow Foucault's lead in examining the "range of subjects to be learned, the functions of the knowing subject and the investment in knowledge...; the way in which knowledge is employed in society, the way it is exploited, divided, and ... attributed" (p. 219), attending also to when and how changes in these aspects occur in American history.

Ab initio

Historians of the Revolutionary period in America have often asserted the influence of classical culture and literature on the Founders. Richard (1994), referencing Commager, summarizes the general opinion that the founding fathers of America recognized more of themselves and their fledgling empire in classical culture than they did in the British one that was their progenitor. The study of classical languages and literature had firmly-established roots in traditional European education and government, and the early American élite took the tradition of classical study with them into the New World, albeit with new interpretations and ideas (Pearcy, 2005). In classical authors, architecture and personae, the Founders identified Greek and Roman connections to their own cultural essence, in language, principles and ideals (Richard, 1994; Winterer, 2002). Their connections to Classics extended beyond anachronistic imitation or interpretation of the ways and words of the ancient ones, a reverence for the *mos maiores*. The men of their social class—élite, influential and powerful—embraced a transmutation of classical ideas and ideals that would find its embodiment in identifiably American concepts of thought, words and actions.

It is useful at this point to refer to Foucault's (1969/1972) description of discursive formations and of the use of his ideas about discourse analysis in examining the establishment and use of classical languages for the development of power and the powerful. Foucault defines discourse as the understandings that emerge in a culture, in given eras, that are comprised of statements about what is possible to know, what is possible to think. Discourse is created by the productive power of knowledge, which is in a reflexive relationship with the dominant or sovereign power (Foucault, 1969/1972). The interaction between power and knowledge emerges in and is created by discourses that appear in many fields, cultural and social arenas. Foucault's concept of "archeology" is a method for excavating and analyzing the elements that discourse creates; namely, the object, subjects, concepts and strategic choices that create the fabric of an historical period. Archeology eschews traditional notions of history, such as temporal or thematic linearity of events, successions, and evolutions, in favor of discovering the power-knowledge connection with discourse. As Foucault explains,

> *L'archéologie ... distingue, dans l'épaisseur même du discours, plusieurs plans d'événements possibles: plan des énoncés eux-mêmes dans leur émergence singulière; plan de l'apparition des objets, des types d'énonciation, des concepts, de choix stratégiques; plan de la dérivation de nouvelles règles de formation...; en fin..., plan où s'effectue la substitution d'une formation discursive à une autre.* (Foucault, 1969, p. 223)

> Archaeology ... distinguishes, within the very thickness of discourse, several levels of possible events: the level of statements themselves in their unique emergence; the level of the appearance of objects, of types of enunciations, of concepts, of strategic choices; the level of the derivation of new rules of

formation...; and finally..., the level where the substitution of one discursive formation for another is effected.

As Winterer (2002) explains in her study of Classicism from 1780 to 1910, preoccupation with classical antiquity came over to America with the colonists from Europe, who believed that the heart of civility, morality and erudition was to be found in the literature and culture of the ancient Romans and Greeks. In the seventeenth and eighteenth centuries, a man who would be responsible for the leadership of others, whether in a governmental position or as religious leader, was required to have been deeply educated in classical languages and literature (primarily Latin, Greek, and Hebrew; other classical languages were rarely, if at all, studied). A century earlier, education in Latin and Greek was primarily seen as preparation for religious leadership, and colleges produced schoolmasters who initially would teach children, with the intention of eventually finding their way into the ministry. Religion maintained control over a population that had shunned monarchy and had found (or interpreted) moral truths in the pagan literature that solidified the connection between Classics and Christianity (Shields, 2001).[6] In Revolutionary and antebellum America, those who would establish democracy found their moral and political inspiration in the Classics.

Although the idea that the Christian colonists found a source of morality in what they understood of the pagan Romans seems paradoxical from a modern standpoint, it is reconcilable from a Foucauldian perspective. Early American colonists lived within the directive that the means to understanding the truths constructed in their time was by way of a long-established tradition of study in classical languages and literature, which contained the rules and structures for living a proper life. Through the ability to read classical literature, an American could know what was necessary to rule, and hence to uphold the truths that they lived by, truths that protected and enacted power and knowledge that characterized life lived well in America. As Pearcy (2005) writes, Classics "had provided the language, tropes and material of public discourse and cultural dialogue" (p. 73).

The establishment of public Latin grammar schools in Massachusetts in the late seventeenth century provided education for a new breed of American aristocracy—one which could read and write in English as well as Latin, Greek, and Hebrew, which could thwart the evil that ignorance of and illiteracy in Biblical and classical texts might breed, and which could ultimately lead the fledgling nation (Pearcy, 2005; Richard, 1998). Following Massachusetts' lead, grammar schools were established throughout the colonies. Not all students were able or required to attend, but those who did and who were determined to be among the best and brightest students were educated with the intention of being prepared to attend college (Winterer, 2002). Watzke (2003) points out that the development of the Latin grammar schools was concurrent with the other development in public elementary education: the town schools. Town schools were established as an alternative to the Latin grammar schools, providing basic elementary education, including, in some instances, foreign language education.[7] At this point, education provided the disciplinary structure as an exercise of power that created subjects—the "educated American"—using an interplay of classics and Protestant Christianity (Shields, 2001; Winterer, 2002).

Eventually, in the early part of the eighteenth century, education in Classics became part of (and was in part responsible for) the *auctoritas* of the political leader, as career paths of college graduates shifted from the ministry to government (Winterer, 2002). Classical ideals, interpreted by the founders who read both Greek and Latin literature, were considered useful for the development of American intellectual capacity and political power. Winterer's words recall Foucault's vision of the dynamic between power, knowledge and discourse when she states that the classically-educated lawyers who would become America's political leaders "hitched literature to politics, words to action, and knowledge to liberty" (p. 17). Foucault (1969) describes the *"cercles concentriques"* in which concepts within literature, words and knowledge become means by which the power-knowledge dynamic emerges in and is transformed by society. He illustrates the circuitous path from knowledge to ideas to discourse:

> *[L'histoire des idées] ... montre comment le savoir scientifique donne lieu à des philosophiques, et prend forme* éventuellement *dans des oeuvres littéraires; ... thèmes peuvent émigrer du champ philosophique où ils ont été formulés ver des discours scientifiques ou politiques.* (Foucault, 1969, p. 180)

> [The history of ideas] ... shows how scientific knowledge brings forth philosophies, and eventually takes form in literary works; themes are able to emigrate from the field of philosophy where they were formulated toward scientific or political discourse.

Using Foucault's methodology, it is possible to view the seventeenth and early eighteenth century as a period in which the dominance of religion as the sovereign power in early America produced the discursive statements that constructed the equation of ignorance and illiteracy with dangerous immorality. Statements that established the concept of immorality also constituted discourses surrounding classical "training"[8] as a means of ameliorating the deficiencies of individuals determined to be educable subjects, and ultimately, auctors who would ensure the place of the moral in society, and thereby enact the existent power dynamics in society. Puritanical condemnation of the lack in the moral fiber of individuals, and concerns about the dangers in the nascent society, would persist until the mid-1700s, when they were supplanted by a political, revolutionary ideology, fueled in part by the movement toward an educated, "thinking" society that would challenge the ministry's dominance (Winterer, 2002, p. 16).

One of the most evanescent yet pervasive concepts in American society is the notion of liberty, and Foucault's explanation of the history of ideas helps to illuminate how this abstraction itself mutates within and subsequently effects changes at certain points in the history of America. For the early Americans, liberty existed as an idea, a discourse, that grounded them, individually as well as collectively, in every aspect of existence, from political action to prayer, from education to exploration, in their personal and social values (Widmer, 2008). Liberty was intricately woven into religion, as de Tocqueville (1904) noted. "The Americans combine the notions of Christianity and of liberty so intimately in their minds that it is impossible to make them conceive the one without the other" (p. 329). Religion served, according to de Tocqueville, as a "governor," a force that could limit the inclination toward excess, immorality, and other dangerous tendencies in a free society. Liberty was also an opposing force to oppression, and the earliest colonists had sought to establish a "New World" founded ostensibly upon the rejection of oppression.

Through the interaction of the ideal of liberty and the grounding of their religion in Protestantism and Calvinist ideology (at least in New England), American colonists inaugurated in their new society a paradigm of domination and oppression, trading religious persecution by the sovereigns and the Roman Catholic Church of the Old World for a "Revolution" that spawned systems of domination over the self, over others, and over physical territory in the New World. Earliest American history demonstrates in many ways the working of this cycle: the domination over the self and its urges or dangerous inclinations, using the religious practices to oppress the self; the domination of others, including native Americans and colonists who were seen to behave in ways that threatened the religious life of the communities; the domination over physical territory, as exhibited in the development of towns and cities, the introduction of nonnative species to the regions in which they lived, and the discursive inevitability of the concept of Manifest Destiny (Widmer, 2008).

To reinforce this cycle of oppression and domination, Americans in the seventeenth, eighteenth and nineteenth centuries had two tools: the Bible and the Classics. Both provided the means to becoming educated and the rationale for domination. From a Foucauldian perspective, both provided knowledge and truths that mechanized power structures. The classical models were not incompatible, but rather complementary, with Christian models. Just as it was possible for Christian and pagan morals to be linked in the American mind, so the linking of religion and liberty was also conceivable during this era (Shields, 2001; Winterer, 2002). The discourse surrounding separation of church and state, which generations of Americans understood to be a fundamental tenet of the new democracy, had not yet evinced itself in the political reality of eighteenth century, if indeed it ever has; one need only to read the orations and political speeches from this era forward, into the twentieth century, to find references to divine "Providence" as guiding efforts and achievements of Americans, or diatribes about the immorality of non-Christian faiths and the governments that operate under their aegis (Widmer, 2008).

Imperium sine fine

The political and economic differentiation by region that accompanied expansion into the western frontier influenced Thomas Jefferson's vision of self-sufficient American citizens, who would ultimately achieve success in the "noble experiment" in self-governance. The emergence of the ideal of democratic thought and classical liberal ideology necessitated, at least in Jefferson's mind, a societal commitment to free and public education. Classical liberalism, with its philosophical commitment to faith in reason, natural law, republican virtue, progress, nationalism and freedom, was the discourse through which the founders gave voice and action to their classical knowledge (Tozer, Violas, & Senese 2002). Since intellectual freedom was essential to the "pursuit of happiness" (which was central to Jefferson's philosophy), achievement of democracy and the safeguarding of liberties for the people required free and open debate on critical issues, from which "truth," which was absolute and unchanging, awaiting discovery by humans, would ultimately emerge. In this way, people would be able to develop their moral and rational capacities, for the benefit of the individual and of society as a whole. Free and open debate required that every man have access to newspapers (as the vehicle for information and instruction), and that every man be able to read them. For Jefferson, literacy and "enlightenment of the masses" through education (at least for white men) was essential to democracy and governance. Jefferson did not include slaves or women in his educational vision, nor did he intend for all white male citizens to receive an equal education (Meckler, 2006; Tozer et al., 2002).[9]

Jefferson and many of his contemporaries believed that the Classics could nurture the political and moral character of those who could and would lead the nation, that the canon of what was considered at that time the essential Classical literature[10] would provide the models for personal behavior and societal structures, including governance (Richard, 1994, p. 53). As Winterer (2002) points out, despite many attacks from such Revolutionary luminaries as Benjamin Franklin, Thomas Paine, and Benjamin Rush regarding the relevance and utility of learning classical languages to the "farmers, mechanics, and merchants," the study of classical history and literature remained important sources for "lessons" in governance, in "the rise, progress and fall of ... nations." (Rush, 1791, as cited in Winterer, 2002, p. 43). In this way, a truly "American" revolution, with the ideal of the American citizen, would be born from the discursive power enacted by the "culturism" of Classics, at least from the perspective of a majority of the Founders. The reality was that Classics, rather than representing a solid structure for the creation of American truths, was vulnerable to the resistance that the enactment of its own power ultimately created, as the self-governing, self-made Americans began to establish their own truths about America.

Richard (1994) cites the work of the Roman historian Tacitus as particularly inspiring—indeed, as nearly oracular—in its effect on the Founders' conception of the content and form of freedom, liberty and government. However, as many of the writings of Jefferson and Adams reveal, confidence in the models and messages of the classical authors was neither absolute nor enduring, and for some (such as Benjamin Rush), they were irrelevant, particularly as compared to those of Christianity (Richard, 2009). Winterer notes that, at the end of the eighteenth century, classical education that had focused so extensively on the grammatical aspects of Latin and Greek had not kept up with the changes in modern society. She states that the pedagogical goals of American classics teachers to "mold gentlemen, ministers who could intelligently read the Bible, and citizens who were moral and dutiful" in a society in which boys were "neither interested in nor good at learning languages" loosened the foundation that classics had originally created in education (Winterer, 2002, p. 43).

Concomitant with the growth in physical territory that America experienced in the early nineteenth century was the movement of much of the existing American populace from the field to the city, a burgeoning immigrant population, and the rapid growth of industry. Tozer et al. (2002) describe the effect that industrialization and the establishment of the factory had in the evolution of an "industrial morality," and the "displacement of a traditional culture with a modern culture" (p. 53). Rhetoric regarding the dissolution of the social fabric and an increase in moral dissipation that accompanied this expansion flourished. Increasingly, social conflict and industrialization provided the impetus for school reform, and mass public education was promoted as the antidote for social disharmony and for training an industrial work force (Reese, 2005; Tozer, et al., 2002). Public education came into its own as a vehicle for achieving and ensuring dominance of business concerns and politicians over the increasing number of subgroups, and of promoting the concept of nationalism and the creation of "the American."

In Foucauldian terms, public schooling thus provided a technology for political domination through discipline and control through objectives directed toward the governmentality of the citizen base. Educating an "ignorant" population, comprised in part by "other"—immigrants, particularly—became an integral focus of an élite who created and were created by the maintenance of increasing power over the American experiment in democratic governance. Whereas the notion of the "uneducated" or "ignorant" person in the seventeenth or early eighteenth century might have referred to the lack of skills needed to read and write for the purpose of engaging in or carrying out religious practices and participation in the new democracy (Vinovskis, 1998), foundational knowledges in the nineteenth century and forward incorporated the power of production, the productivity of the individual on behalf of the larger concern, be it for industrial or governmental, academic or civic production. As the industrial revolution took hold in America, industry required a populace educated in manual arts, masses of skilled workers to stoke the fires of manufacturing that would propel an emergent capitalist economy, of people "schooled" in the capacity to follow directions and to work as a unit (Reese, 2005; Tozer et al., 2002). As centralized government control became a more complex issue, with local, state and federal levels of government and industry engaged in a dance not unlike future attempts to determine where power and control did or should exist, the requirement of the American democracy of the period was of a functionally literate citizenry who could and would participate in the workings of politics.

The enhancement of individual lives through the rules and controls set forth in education was viewed as a means of ameliorating urban problems and for creating a spirit of nationalism, an allegiance to "Americanism." Local control over schooling began to yield to more centralized governmental control over schooling (Tozer et al., 2002). In this environment, classical education met a much larger and more diverse student population, and with that diversity came ideological and practical changes in the discourse about the purposes and place of Latin and Greek in the secondary school classrooms, and in higher education. The extent to which the skills and values that the Founders believed were inherent in classical learning were compatible with the practical needs of this growing population came into serious question. The nature of the "self-evident truths" of the "Declaration of Independence" which the Founders had signed took on a different meaning, and the notion of freedom was increasingly subject to what the wealthy and powerful in government and business were willing or able to provide during the industrialization of America. Tozer et al.

describe the shift in the concept of freedom in this era from the classical liberal construction as "negative freedom," that is, freedom as a result of lack of government interference, to a modern liberal belief in freedom as constituted by greater power being given to government to protect freedom by regulating society, a notion of "positive freedom" (p. 103).

However, Foucault (2000) reminds us that "relations of power...necessarily extend beyond the limits of the state.... The state can only operate on the basis of other, already existing power relations" (pp. 122-123). The question of what mattered in education, of whose knowledge was important at this juncture refers us back to the paradigm of dominance over self, other, and the environment discussed earlier. The language, knowledge and culture of the immigrant populations was not only unimportant to the growing industrial complex; in order to promote the sustainability of industrialization and Americanization of the populace, the state was required to ensure the oppression of the "original" cultural selves of the people. As Ransom (1993) notes, immigration and the increase of the "foreign population" was viewed by many Americans who considered themselves "native-born" (by virtue of their birth having taken place in America, despite the likelihood that their not-so-distant ancestors had been born elsewhere) as the cause of burgeoning poverty and crime in the cities, and immigrants were expected to cast off their "customs, habits and languages" of the countries from which they had come and "imbue themselves with American feelings" (Ransom, citing a article in *The New York Times* written in 1854, p. 133). Education was the mechanism by which this could be accomplished (Tozer et al., 2002), and thus education that was organized as a "disciplinary" institution, in Foucauldian terms, to ensure the development of compliant people with a scope of limited scope of knowledge appropriate to the needs of the powerful. Functional literacy and numeracy were relevant and useful to the needs of industry, and necessary for the "normalization" (again, Foucault's term), even "Americanization," of a diverse population.

Classical cultural models and education increasingly appeared to have relevance for none but the academy-bound in the nineteenth century. Despite the political expedience that being familiar with classical languages and literature had for the American élite who wished to communicate with the European élite (Pearcy, 2005, p.67), there was no guarantee that, once they got to the halls of higher education, there would be universal agreement about the role that their knowledge would play in their future careers. Although most of government's leaders were likely to have had substantial background in Classics, changes in requirements of colleges, which in many cases eliminated the requirement of classical languages for entrance into or for graduation from some colleges (Harvard, under Charles Eliot, among them), meant that, by the 61st Congress in

1910, many Senators may have had little knowledge of Classics (Meckler, 2006). The ability to read Latin, to quote Cicero or Sallust, or to apply the lessons of ancient history to contemporary events became little more than ornamentation in the oratory of the powerful (Winterer, cited in Meckler, 2006). Illiteracy in the Classics was no longer equated with ignorance, and it even became possible to use one's lack of such knowledge as an appeal to the common man.

A shift was also occurring in the paradigm within which those who were in charge of the perpetuation of Classics in America functioned. As Winterer (2002) describes it, classical studies moved "from words to worlds": a shift from almost exclusive study of grammar to a much broader exploration of cultural and historical aspects of Greece and Rome, and from a model that embraced ancient Rome (which Winterer traces as an Enlightenment tendency to view Roman history as a mirror of contemporary American struggles), toward a model that used the ideal of Greek culture as a reflection of the new faith in a progressive improvement of the individual and society (p. 81). This recalls Foucault's (1969/1972) notion of discourses re-forming or being modified in education as appropriate, according to the knowledge and power they bring with them. As Americans became more interested in the ideal of the "self-made man" (Henry Clay's term, as cited in Winterer, 2002, p. 81), Classics provided a new path to the improvement or development of the self, through the self-examination that they encountered in Greek tragedies, in Demosthenes, and in Homer, in ways that were complementary to, though also constrained by, Christian faith.

Winterer (2002) also traces the changes in the idea of culture, beginning in the 1850s, in which the "cultivation" of the mind, tastes and broad knowledge of the student became a pedagogical goal that could counter the marginalization of Classics in the face of increased focus on the "utility" of knowledge (p. 82). While there may have been little argument about the importance of Classical education for development of erudition and culture in college students, the question of Classics' utility in education came into serious question in public secondary education, and, as a consequence, into the bulwark of liberal education: the colleges and universities. The notion of production became an issue in academia as well, as the growth of the university and an American version of scholarship implied that the war for independence had been fought in the intellectual battlefields as well. The desire to establish high-quality American scholarship was exceptionally keen in Classics; it would not be until the early twentieth century that American classicists would be able to assert with great confidence that they had produced a quantity of scholars and studies that could effectively challenge European, particularly German, scholars in depth and breadth of quality in classical studies (Pearcy, 2005; Winterer, 2002).[11]

In 1827, Yale College established a committee to evaluate the course of study it would require of students in its design of a "liberal education" examining specifically whether to keep Latin and Greek ("the dead languages") as requirements for admission or to leave them out altogether (*Yale Report of 1828*, p. 31). The writers of the *Yale Report of 1828* contended in their advocacy of retaining requirements in Latin and Greek in the college curriculum as the foundation of liberal education, that the colleges could not reliably continue to educate students in the classical tradition if precollege education did not include education in Latin and Greek. Despite a renewed focus in Classics based on the premise that the study of classical cultures had a key, and necessary, role in creating an idealistic view of the potential of American culture, and despite a new interest in a broader view of Classics in the universities, which now included the development of archaeology and scholarship that could compete with European (particularly German) models, the stature of Classics in the mid-1800s was threatened on two important fronts: the new interest in science and scientific models as purveyors of truths, and the inability of classic education to help people to resolve the issue of slavery. In no way, as Winterer points out (in Meckler, 2006), could the Hellenism of the nineteenth century unite individual and public sentiment over the volatile and inevitable issue of slavery in America.

Multa quoque et bello passus

The Civil War and its aftermath mark a Foucauldian "historical rupture," a point at which divergences from what had been the dominant power-knowledge-truth structure would occur. Critical questions about the nature of domination and oppression were asked in earnest, fueled by the issue of slavery, but extending into the religious, ethnic, and political ideals held by each region. Morality became the province of those who found slavery untenable, yet also of those who, through a literal reading of the Bible, justified slavery through the words of their God and in the "unalienable rights" set forth in the Declaration of Independence (Ransom, 1993).

The development of "America" and the "American" had been largely a history of domination, oppression and reinvention of self, other, and physical territory. The very forces that had enacted these dominations and oppressions came into conflict with each other in the mid-1850s, including the struggle for economic and political power, and caused differences between the North and the South to caused critical voices to come to the fore. This turmoil, the culmination of which was represented by the Civil War, thoroughly rocked the foundation of America. The core of Republicanism, with its ideal of "liberation of the masses" from the old forms of truth and domination, was still present, but new forms were taking shape. Just as the Civil War forced America to consider a revised concept of "union," "freedom," and the value of "rebellion" in the face of the glaring contradictions that boiled up in the conflict, a revolution in public education was also taking place. Enrollments in public schools increased substantially from the mid-1800s through the early decades of the twentieth century (Reese, 2005), and new ideas about the purposes of education produced new forms of domination, mostly formed by ideas of capitalism and "the market" (Reese, 2005; Tozer et al., 2002). Among the previously-dominant ideas that changed in the mid-nineteenth century was the relevance of the Classics, classical models, and classical education for the American state. The faith in the Classics and classical education as a source of truth and power was supplanted by the new domination of science and the utility of knowledge.

In the post-Civil War period, the embrace of science as the dominant way of knowing, of accessing truths and of generating power structures resulted in dynamic changes in systems of knowledge, learning and education. Winterer (2002) describes the impact of this period on classical education and scholarship in the last third of the nineteenth century as the "historical moment when learning began to splinter into two worlds, the world of specialized 'scientific' scholarship and the world of cultivated generalism" (p. 154). This splinter could be seen as an aftershock, or an echo, from the chasm that was created at the Mason-Dixon line, and its effects were demonstrated in the shift from Classics as defining civic responsibility to creating the private culture or cultivation of the American citizen (Winterer, 2002, p. 142). Prior to the war, the North and South had already begun to use classical tradition in ways that helped to define differences in the regional beliefs, particularly in the way in which the South characterized the northern competitive, materialist "modernity" in contrast to the southern agrarian, slave society, justified by classical models in Rome and Athens (p. 77). In addition, the growth of a middle class that had access to classical literature and which purchased images (in paintings, cheap figurines, and other household fixtures) emphasized the link between Classics and "class," or high culture, at the same time that the link to Classics and political culture and power was disintegrating (p. 142).

There were several final blows dealt to classical education in the late nineteenth century that effectively removed the Classics from the center of power structures in the political and educational arenas of America. Meckler (2006) connects the rise in populism in government with the decline of classical education, as he traces a path from the call for more public involvement (especially by those groups that business and elite society had marginalized or abused) to the establishment of the Seventeenth Amendment to the U.S. Constitution, which called for a direct election of United States senators, to the perception by the general public that classical education was the luxury of the élite. In addition, as Meckler (2006) points out, leaders in business viewed Classics as utterly irrelevant to the success and power of their enterprises. Classics was no longer a prerequisite for a economically successful life, as many powerful industrial magnates had demonstrated. The power/knowledge structure in American education had shifted from classical knowledge as productive of truths and power to new paradigms. One was the advent of specialization of knowledge into separate disciplines, replacing the idea of broad, general knowledge as the foundation for the educated person and the qualified élite. As the drive toward specialization occurred, notions about the value of certain disciplines or specialties over others also surfaced; for example, English replaced Classics as the prominent study in Humanities (Winterer, 2002), and natural sciences were perceived as more practically useful than the Humanities. Specialization also took Classics in new directions toward the development of a more scientific study of Classics that would firmly ensconce it (and eventually, the rest of the humanities) in the realm of the increasingly élitist Academy, where "cultivated erudition" (Winterer's term) could live its decidedly undemocratic life in relative isolation from the broader concerns of American capitalism.

In an era that had essentially deified science, even in a society that had never lost its attachment to religion, the general knowledge that traditional paths in classical education provided was subordinated to the expertise and empiricism of scientific knowledge (Tozer et al., 2002). The knowledge of science was productive, both in terms of physical evidence of science in action and from a Foucauldian view of the power it produced. The role of science was construed as constructive; it created power, used power and was created and used by the powerful, who could look to the truths borne out by science to justify virtually any act, authority, or belief (the oppression of slavery, the dominance of intelligence over perceived ignorance, etc.).

As a response to the new dominance of science and specialization, new types of scholarship grew in classical studies at universities, including forays into science through archaeology, and professional study of specialized antiquities. As a result, two new professional societies were established: the American Philological Association (the APA) in 1869, and the Archaeological Institute of America (AIA) in 1879. In some respects, the AIA, and archaeology, as the new science of Classics, had a wider appeal to the American public than did the rather esoteric studies that became the province of the APA, as the "professionalized" arm of Classics. At the very least, the science of archaeology, already flourishing in Europe in the wake of the dramatic excavations of classical sites in the Mediterranean, captivated the American imagination and competitive spirit. It is important to note that, in its early days, the AIA espoused as superior the value of classical archaeological excavations, and disregarded indigenous American sites as elements of an insignificant "prehistory"[12] of a savage, crude civilization that had nothing to do with the origins of the sophisticated American culture that had its roots in the high cultures of ancient Greece and Rome.

The APA, in its first meeting in 1869, was somewhat less restrictive, including discussions and paper presentations on nonclassical languages, including some native American languages. Presentations on the indigenous languages were rather narrowly focused, however—mostly philological in nature, they compared the language systems of those languages to English, but several also dealt with issues of the means of preserving indigenous North and South American languages.[13] The range of papers and discussions on the topics considered in this new convention is fairly wide; the record of the initial proceedings detail the participants' exploration of linguistics, pedagogy in classical and modern languages, and, first and foremost, philology and comparative philology. The APA envisioned itself as "a working society ... worth what it brings forth for universal use" (Hurlburt, 1869). Society members were charged with a critical responsibility to the preservation (through philology) of indigenous languages. "Our duty to the races whom we are dispossessing and destroying makes American philology and archaeology our especial responsibility, and it is our disgrace as a nation that we have been unfaithful to it" (p. 31). The acknowledgement of this "national disgrace" was in sharp contrast to the unmitigated and intentional destruction of Native Americans that was a hallmark of American imperialistic expansion. This position, a fairly unusual one from an organization associated with the production of élite knowledge, might have had greater impact had the society's chief emphasis transcended the "scientification" of its focus. The perceived threat to Classics as an educational foundation from the increased emphasis on the sciences stands out in the pages of the proceedings of the first and second sessions, with numerous comparisons made to the effectiveness of Classics in providing the general public with the "best education for their circumstances." Referencing the "New Education," one member recounted three kinds of education that were suited to the American "favored few:" practical, scientific and classical, which worked in tandem to secure the ends of education, including the "development of intellectual power, the us[e] of that power, and the capacity of ... labor directed to worthy objects" (as cited in Hurlburt, p. 17). All of these things, he said, were available in classical education; in no way could scientific education achieve these goals. At the same time that these classicists attempted to secure Classics' position at the head of the academy, they assured its increased isolation from general society.

The geopolitical complex that emerged with the advent of the First World War effectively removed classical languages from the arsenal in the stronghold of general education. Finally, perhaps permanently, Classics found itself relegated to the margins, available only to certain students, even though several reports from this era attempt to downplay the exodus of students in secondary schools from classes in Latin and Greek. Classical languages were subordinated to certain European modern languages in practical importance, and knowledge of "other" or "foreign" languages represented a new path to American domination in the world. International conflicts presented a convenient rationale for study of these languages by Americans, but the utility of the knowledge of European languages—most importantly French and Spanish—was not entirely related to the goal of communication as it was as a foundation for domination.[14] Some modern languages – particularly German, faced elimination from public education primarily on the basis of wartime xenophobia, and the effect of the fall of German and the rise of French and Spanish (as more politically appropriate languages for American students to study) was concomitant with a significant change in the rationale and pedagogical goals of foreign language education in public secondary schools (see Watzke, 2003). As educational goals shifted from earlier emphases on preparation for participation in politics and society to a focus on the development of life skills and vocational training, language education was viewed as largely superfluous, lacking relevance for what students would need to learn to function well in U.S. society (Watzke, 2003). New educational models worked against both modern language and classical education as well. Thorndike's efficiency model sounded the death-knell for classical education in the secondary schools. Classics no longer represented a key to the grammar of our civility—its moral codes did not matter any longer. Arguments for the benefits of classical language learning in assisting in the growth of the mind and development of habits of learning were not as persuasive to the college-bound as they had previously been.[15] The rise of behaviorism meant a rejection of the idea of "transfer of training," which had provided intellectual support for the study of the Classics. In this culture of political expediency and economic focus, secondary schools found other disciplines that could foster the kind of knowledge that could ostensibly contribute to America's success on the world's military stage. The critical thinking that previous generations had believed classical studies could inspire was actually counter to what the dynamic interaction of power-knowledge-truth held in the 1920s onward. Increasingly, the truths of sciences were emphasized as the means for the growth of American power in the world.

After the Second World War, the United States found itself presumably at the figurative top of the world, having experienced the most growth in territory and power of any new nation that had emerged in 300 years. Competition and capitalism became concepts almost as captivating to the American mind as liberty had been. Liberty still guided the American spirit (or so the discourse ran), but capitalism and the new idea of a competitive global market now drove the power/knowledge/truths structure. In education, business models imprinted on the classroom the disciplinary ideas about efficiency, productivity, and relevance of education to the workplace and global competitiveness of Americans and America. Emphases in natural sciences and social sciences required more time in the curricula established in secondary schools and colleges. Advances in sciences prompted the call for more math and science courses in schools, which effected a reduction of the amount of time and focus devoted to humanities. Modern languages (primarily European, and especially Spanish—see Watzke, 2003) were increasingly viewed as more relevant than classical, in the belief that it was necessary for Americans to communicate in international political and economic arenas. English still took precedent over any foreign language, as the new "default humanity" (Winterer, 2002), and as part of the domination and dominion that America continues still to try to enact over the globe.

Pearcy (2005) traces part of the failure of Classics to thrive in America to the efforts of classical philologists who attempted to "convert the study of languages into a science," losing the interest of those who believed in the cultural and cultivating value of classics and thus ensuring the place of classical studies at the margins of liberal education (p. 82). In addition, as Pearcy contends, the inability of Classics to find a truly American voice meant that as soon as the forces of power, knowledge and truth were no longer enacted by Classics, there was little room in the exercise of American power for Classics.

Ad nostra tempora

Considered to be the *sine qua non* of the highly-educated person until the early part of the twentieth century, the ability to read Latin and Greece has in the past several decades become a skill relegated to the outermost margins of curricula in secondary schools; within the still-elective study of foreign languages in America, Latin and Greek programs continue to be lightly populated in public schools. A resurgence in Latin programs at the high school level that began in the mid-1990s (LaFleur, 1998) seemed to indicate that Americans were not yet ready to eliminate classical languages entirely from the curricula, but that resurgence peaked in 2000, and there has been little or no growth in the number of students taking Latin in recent years.[16] Classics' hold on the tiny corner it occupies in American education remains tenuous at best, as its image as a useful and relevant course of study, in an era that still embraces utility and relevance as the predominant discourse in education, continues to wane.

Despite the decline of interest and availability of classical subjects and learning in American public schools, there is still a curiously anachronistic presence of classical images and reconceptions of the ancient Roman and Greek worlds in popular culture. Hollywood has embraced the epic and heroic tales of the classical era for decades, and in the last 10 years, several movies have been produced that put a particularly twenty-first century face on legendary and historical figures from Greece and Rome in productions such as *Gladiator, Troy, Alexander, 300,* and the semipornographic *Caligula*.[17] Longer series made for television, such as PBS's *I, Claudius* and Home Box Office's (HBO) series *Rome,* dramatized the political and social scene in during the late Republic and early Empire periods in ancient Rome. It is worth mentioning that the latter program (*Rome,* which aired for two seasons) demonstrated a substantial investment of time and money by producers in the research on this time period, to create as authentic a production as possible.

Beyond popular entertainment, Classics continues to thrive in caricature. In American politics, the neoconservatives appeared to have co-opted Plato as their spokesman (based on the reported connections between the teachings of political philosopher Leo Strauss and members of the Bush administration—see Robertson, in Meckler, 2006). Madison Avenue and corporate America continues its love affair with Greco-Roman "culture," as evidenced by the numerous references to mythological places and figures, the appearance of toga-clad characters in advertisements, and even some Latin—the athletic shoe company ASICS's name is an acronym for the Latin phrase *"anima sana in corpore sano,"* adapted from the Roman poet Juvenal, which they revealed in a recent television commercial. Although such use of Classics is not necessarily relevant to the history of classical education in America, it is still an interesting paradox that contemporary concepts of "usefulness" of classical images, languages, and ideas in the products of modern popular culture assumes a degree of familiarity with the Greeks and Romans in an era that may eventually see education in Classics cease to exist.

Arguments abound regarding the place that Classical education should occupy in American education, and those arguments have changed little since the post-Civil War era. Scholars, educators, and policymakers have debated for nearly 200 years about the relevance of classical education, about the "deadness" of Latin and Greek languages, and the pedagogical concepts that result from the attempt to teach within these constructive notions. In the late twentieth century, the problems surrounding these issues had not abated. LaFleur, in his 1987 study of the teaching of Latin, outlined educational trends of the past 40 to 50 years that he connected with the precipitous drops in student enrollment. He alluded to the "Decade of the Relevant," between 1960 and 1970, when "Johnny did his thing ... then forgot how to read and write," and SAT verbal scores correspondingly plummeted (LaFleur, p. 2). LaFleur discussed the 79% drop in Latin enrollments (from 1962 to 1976) in the context of the demand for relevancy, the de-emphasis of Latin in the Roman Catholic Church after Vatican II, the abandonment of a core curriculum, and the "cafeteria-line" approach to graduation requirements. "Latin," he wrote, "that most ancient of relics, was first to go" (p. 3). He also reported another trend that continues to plague existing Latin programs, primarily in secondary schools: the dearth of qualified Latin teachers, a result of the decline in interest and the subsequent reduction in graduates from university programs in Classics.

Many recent articles and books have been written that argue that more curriculum, more time, and more study of classical languages, history and culture benefits individuals and American society. *The New York Times* published an op-ed article by Harry Mount, a journalist whose recent book, *Carpe diem: Put a Little Latin in Your Life*, became a best seller. Mount's (2007) editorial reiterated his claims that everyone would be better off knowing at least some Latin, and that leaders in the U.S. would particularly benefit (if only by being able to avoid grammatical gaffes that characterized Bush soundbites), but the more noteworthy aspect of the article is that it prompted many readers to comment rather vigorously for and against education in classical languages and culture.

That so much discussion exists and that there is such difference of opinion is at least a sign that Classics is worth arguing about. In some respects, the tenor of these debates has not largely changed much in the last two centuries. Americans have been surprisingly reluctant to allow classical education to fully perish, and instead have consistently pondered its usefulness for their society and its students, weighing the efficacy of education Latin and Greek against modern (generally European) languages, and classical pedagogy against more modern techniques for learning language. The ripple effect of those conflicts, especially those surrounding pedagogical practices, reached into the secondary school classrooms. The battle raged (and has not abated in recent decades) among advocates of grammar study and translation "method" of instruction in Latin (and Greek, which was rarely taught in American high schools, and almost never in elementary schools) and the so-called "reading method," in which students read full passages written in Latin from the first day of instruction, and also among advocates of an immersion model of instruction, in which students and teachers explore Latin as a spoken language, using techniques similar to those used in many modern-language classrooms.

The dominant ideologies of the modern era, including the supremacy of science and reliance on experts as the purveyors of truth, the pursuit of human efficiency and predictability, competition and the concomitant notion of relativity in civic morality have affected Classics' role in education in practical, observable ways. The discussion concerning the effectiveness of language pedagogies in the classical language classroom can be traced in the United States from the latter-half of the nineteenth century, from the earliest transcripts of the APA (American Philological Association), which sought to support an "American" conception of Classicism to the 1930s and 1940s, as foreign language education came to be viewed as necessary to U.S. success in wartime, to the present. Throughout this time period, and increasingly so in the late twentieth to early twenty-first centuries, secondary school and university teachers have struggled to keep Classics departments with sufficient enrollments and to convince a public that has been focused on the practical utility of education since the advent of industrialization that Classics is still somehow relevant to modern society.

The marginalization of Classics in the twentieth century has created a unique opportunity in the United States, an opportunity that might not have been present in earlier eras, under previous premises about knowledge, power, and truth. As it is itself on the margins of educational power, Classics becomes worthy of critical thinking, thinking about issues of domination, subjugation and oppression. Because it is not expected to yield examples or models for life, we can look at the classical world with new eyes, with critical eyes. We do not need to read Tacitus for his moral guidance; instead, we can read his account of Germania for what it says about how dominant cultures view The Other. We can read Cicero to understand the degree to which he speaks about excluding rather than including, of domination and reaction to the threat of revolt. We can read Vergil, Euripides or Homer to understand the way in which war victimizes the least powerful, and to what lengths men will go to assure domination and dominion over others, and what destiny has to say about it, or to explore the tension between personal goals and desires and civic responsibility. Finally, Classics itself, as it undergoes the trials of self-reflection and reinvention in pedagogy and scholarship through the work of its practitioners, and as its participants explore their potential to become more critically aware, offers a model for those both within and outside of its world.

NOTES

1. Farrell (2001) also cites this passage and treats it similarly in his discussion of the "universality" of Latin culture and the myth of Latin language as a "civilizing force" (pp. 1-3).
2. Shields (2001) also asserts a comparison between George Washington and Aeneas with respect to Washington's *pietas*, an ancient Roman concept of virtue (with no completely suitable English translation) that combines devotion to duty, to fulfillment of one's destiny and to one's family (p. 76).
3. Rush had initially extolled the benefits of classical education, but in his later years had expended considerable effort in writing and oratory to vigorously attack it (Winterer, 2006).
4. My title for this chapter is inspired by Winterer's work (2002).
5. See Shields (2001, p. 76).
6. The Classics had provided such truths for Christian dogma in previous centuries; see, e.g., Plato's influence on the Church in the Byzantine era (Hankins, 1990).
7. Watzke (2003) also discusses a significant difference between the two models regarding language instruction: "When instruction in modern languages took place in town schools, it reflected the ethnic makeup of the community and often was the medium of daily instruction, serving a social and vocational purpose" (p. 2). This provides an interesting point of reflection upon modern language instruction in our own time, especially as the debate about bilingual education continues to flare.
8. A distinction here is made between training as a prescribed means of controlling or disciplining subjects and education, which, proceeding from its Latin roots, refers to a means of bringing forth capacities in individuals. Education is also recognized as a tool for controlling subjects and assuring dominance.
9. Of course, this is consistent with the classical models of domination over women, slaves, children and others.
10. Among the Classical authors Richard (1994) lists as intellectual, moral and political guides for the Founders are Vergil, Cicero, Homer, Hesiod, Sallust, Plutarch, and Xenophon (p. 53); he also reminds us that the Founders considered several legendary characters, such as Cincinnatus and Aeneas, as heroic models. An investigation of these models as metaphors for the Founders' ideal "selves" is beyond the scope of this chapter, but may be useful to consider from a Foucauldian perspective as models of American "truths." See also Ziobro (2006) on the classical curriculum of the early American Latin grammar schools and colleges.
11. Paul Shorey (1919), in his address to the American Philological Association in 1910, made the case that American classicists, in the 50 years prior to his address, had produced more compelling and more relevant studies than had their European counterparts.
12. According to Winterer (2002, p. 140), "prehistory" entered the American vocabulary with the discovery of the first human fossils in the 1860s,

prompting classical scholars to rethink what was previously known of the ancient world through literature alone.

13. See for example, the Hon. J. H. Trumbull of Connecticut, "The True Method of Studying the North American Languages" (pp. 25-26), George Gibbs of New York, "What More Efficient Measures Can Be Taken to Preserve From Destruction the Aboriginal Languages (pp. 27-28), Rev. Thomas Hurlburt of Canada, "On the Structure of Indian Languages" (pp. 26-27) in *Transactions of the American Philological Association (1869-96)*, 1(1869-70).

14. Classical languages were not the only ones subject to negative discourse in America's pursuit of domination in the world. Pavlenko (2003) analyzed arguments made by proponents of policies during the First World War that drastically reduced instruction in German (most significantly during the escalation of the military campaign against Germany) and limited instruction in other languages (including Russian, Japanese, Chinese, and Italian) thought to be lacking in practical value and which they believed had the potential to "contaminate" the moral values of American students.

15. The Yale Report (1828) had defended a commitment to Classics as the center of the curriculum on the basis of its value in understanding the foundations of western civilization, especially elements of "high culture," such as literature and the arts, as preparation for highly skilled professions such as law and medicine, and for its capacity to improve mental discipline. These arguments ultimately were not enough to stave off the decline of classical studies; however, it is interesting to note how often very similar arguments have been used, even in very recent years, to defend Classics in education (e.g., see Henry Mount's article in *The New York Times* in 2007).

16. According to a recent survey conducted by Rhodes and Pufahl (2009), the percentage of secondary schools offering Latin dropped from 20% in 1997 to 13% in 2008, but the percentage of elementary schools increased from 3% in 1997 to 6% in 2008.

17. The historic inaccuracies and misconceptions in these popular interpretations of Classical culture abound, of course. Some are more subtle than others. Perhaps no inaccuracy has been as controversial, however, as the fact that, in Mel Gibson's movie, *The Passion*, the Roman soldiers speak Latin to each other, rather than the *koine* Greek that would have most likely been spoken as a lingua franca in that part of the world in that time (see Adams, 2003, p. 294).

CHAPTER 3

VERITAS

Critical Pedagogy and Reality in the Foreign Language Classroom

οὐ μνημονεύεις, ὦ φίλε, ὅτι ἐγὼ μὲν οὔτ' οἶδα οὔτε ποιοῦμαι τῶν τοιούτων
οὐδὲν ἐμόν, ἀλλ' εἰμὶ αὐτῶν ἄγονος, σὲ δὲ μαιεύομαι καὶ τούτου ἕνεκα ἐπᾴδω
τε καὶ παρατίθημι ἑκάστων τῶν σοφῶν ἀπογεύσασθαι, ἕως ἄν εἰς φῶς τὸ σὸν
δόγμα συνεξαγάγω· ἐξαχθέντος δὲ τότ' ἤδη σκέψομαι εἴτ' ἀνεμιαῖον εἴτε
γόνιμον ἀναφανήσεται. ἀλλὰ θαρρῶν καὶ καρτερῶν εὖ καὶ ἀνδρείως
ἀποκρίνου ἃ ἂν φαίνηταί σοι περὶ ὧν ἂν ἐρωτῶ.

—Plato (Theatetus, 157c-d)[1]

You do not remember, friend that I neither know nothing of these things nor
do I consider any of them as mine; I myself am sterile, but I am midwife to
you of these things, and for that reason I spout questions and I put them to
you and I have given you a bit of each of the theories, until, together with
you, I bring your opinions into the light; having been led out, I will examine
all of it and will see whether a windegg or something worthwhile will blaze
up. But take courage and be patient, and in a good, manly way respond
about what I show to you and what I am asking.

Consiliō et Animīs: Tracing a Path to Social Justice Through the Classics, pp. 43–68
Copyright © 2012 by Information Age Publishing

43

The ancient Greek emphasis on self-reflection comes into our present through the art, philosophy, and literature that has been parsed by generations in the West. Plato, Aristotle, Homer, the great tragedians (Aeschylus, Sophocles, and Euripides) and other writers have offered generations in the West the critical eyes through which we may examine who we are, why we are, and what we do and are not able to do. The Greeks were generally unflinching in their gaze upon the human condition, and rarely did they offer any escape from the realizations which might be most difficult to accept. Homer provided heroes who could never be comfortably idolized—Achilles' self-serving wrath and Odysseus' hubris reminds us that, in the greatest moments of heroism, personal demons and human failings do not lurk far behind. Sophocles' Oedipus saved a city by means of his intellect, but the extent of his wisdom was not sufficient to mitigate his fate or that of his children and subjects. Euripides turned a mirror in our direction; in the reflection, we can see the ease with which we feed the dark side of our tendencies. For example, in the *Trojan Women*, we see that society's acceptance of the subjugation and destruction of the most innocent and vulnerable as a matter of fact in war makes us all slaves to our own aggression. In his *Hippolytus*, Phaedra ruminates:

ἤδη ποτ' ἄλλως νυκτὸς ἐν μακρῷ χρόνῳ
θνητῶν ἐφρόντισ' ᾗ διέφθαρται βίος.
καί μοι δοκοῦσιν οὐ κατὰ γνώμης φύσιν
πράσσειν κάκιον: ἔστι γὰρ τό γ' εὖ φρονεῖν
πολλοῖσιν: ἀλλὰ τῇδ' ἀθρητέον τόδε:
τὰ χρήστ' ἐπιστάμεσθα καὶ γιγνώσκομεν,
οὐκ ἐκπονοῦμεν δ', οἱ μὲν ἀργίας ὕπο,
οἱ δ' ἡδονὴν προθέντες ἀντὶ τοῦ καλοῦ ἄλλην τιν'. (Euripides, *Hippolytus* 374-383)

I have reflected previously, at other times in the long hours of the night, where the lives of mortals are utterly destroyed. To me, it seems that not from the quality of their judgment do they fare badly, for in any case there are many who are prudent. Rather, consider it thus: we are capable of and recognize what is good, but do not complete its work, some on account of laziness, others because they have put pleasure before virtue.

The inability or unwillingness to question, or to see our habits, motivations, and beliefs through a critical lens, has produced tremendous suffering in ourselves and in the world.[2] Socrates, the self-appointed "midwife" of consciousness in young men in ancient Athens, required that individuals question all that they thought of as knowledge, wisdom or truth, in order to seek the greatest Good, and to improve themselves as they functioned in the world. His tool was dialectic, literally, the "sorting through" of the stuff of mind in order to see the difference between knowledge accepted *prima facie*, and understanding through turning knowledge on its head to see the underside that may reverse our concepts of "reality."[3]

Socrates and Michel Foucault might have engaged in some riveting dialectic, for though they used the language of philosophy rather differently, they had in common the impetus to bring to light the "how" and "what" of a society's beliefs and what those produce, and the questioning of the subjective nature of reality. As Socrates points out, even with the use of rational tools such as "those sciences which we have said have an apprehension of being—geometry and the like—are, we see, only dreamings about being. But for them to reveal the full waking reality is impossible, as long as they leave untouched the hypotheses they use, and do not themselves have the ability to tell the full story" (Plato, *Republic*, VII, 527-533). Foucault's (2000) description of truths that arise from society's power/knowledge structures is rather like Socrates' point, and both have strong implications for the social and political present, as well for the individual. Foucault would relate Socrates' "dreamings about being," with their unquestioned assumptions, to the épistémès and discourses of the present. Just as Socrates maintained the importance of a person's inquiry into the nature of reality in order to be freed from the power of illusion or delusion, Foucault also suggested that critical inquiry is essential for transformation in a society: "As soon as people begin to have trouble thinking things the way they have been thought, transformation becomes at the same time very urgent, very difficult, and entirely possible" (p. 457).

Critical pedagogy practitioners and theorists are midwives themselves; they attempt to raise the transformative questions about the status quo in education (as a political entity) that have the potential to benefit students, teachers, and society. Their critical inquiry (and that of their students) has the capacity to create a much richer, more nurturing field in which to sow the seeds of hope, liberty, compassion, and ultimately, social justice. As Paulo Freire (1970) pointed out,

> *A libertação, por isto, é um parto. E um parto doloroso. O homem que nasce deste parto é um homem novo que só é viável na e pela, superação da contradição opressores-oprimidos, que é libertação de todos.* (p. 19)

Thus, liberation is a childbirth. And a painful childbirth. The person who is born from this birth is a new person, who is viable only in and by overcoming the oppressor-oppressed contradiction; that is the liberation of all.

Critical pedagogy has been traditionally associated with educational practices that focus on resistance to the forces of domination and oppression in education and in the world. It has nearly as many facets as it has proponents. Under the critical pedagogy umbrella stand radical pedagogy, revolutionary pedagogy, liberatory pedagogy, feminist pedagogy, queer pedagogy and other approaches to engaging students and teachers in the critical examination of the interplay of politics, economics, ideologies and social relationships and their impact on the acts of teaching, learning, curriculum development, professional development, and the physical structures in which education takes place. While there are many variations in the viewpoints of critical pedagogy, most are grounded in a view of public education and schooling[4] as political and social functions that are central to the culturalization of the masses, as "technologies of a nation…, about the protection and production of its Culture … and the production of its sovereign subjects" (Luke, 2004, p. 24). As such, a critical engagement with educational systems and functions requires that they bear scrutiny, based upon key principles: that social justice and emancipation of the most vulnerable and oppressed in society is central to the purposes and goals of education; that the potential for emancipatory action exists in a cycle of praxis that includes critical reflection, dialogue, and conscientization (a critical social consciousness) in the work of students and teachers that leads to new action; and that the intent of critical learning and teaching is to challenge all forms of oppression or oppressive ideologies (Darder, 2003; Freire, 1970; Giroux, 2003a, 2003b; Kanpol, 1998; Kincheloe, 2008; McLaren, 2003). Critical pedagogy asserts that the mainstream approach to education, with its emphases on technical skills, categorizations and a top-down approach to learning has closed students (and teachers) off from realizing their full potential as liberated beings. Rather than providing a path to liberation, the educational system has historically perpetuated the existence of inequity, imbalance, and oppression in class, race, gender and other relations, in classrooms, schools, and in the world (Freire, 1994; Giroux, 2005; McLaren, 2003).

Critical pedagogy is grounded in the premise that no knowledge, no educational practice, no educational environment, is neutral. As Peter McLaren (2003) states, "There is no 'objective' environment that is not stamped with social presence" (p. 81). Foucault's (2000) description of the "regimes of truth" (p. 132) that emerge from productive power of knowledge is relevant here: "Truth is a thing of this world: it is produced only by virtue of multiple forms of restraint. And it induces regular effects of power." Further, educational "truths"—knowledge (including who possesses it), achievement and measurement, curriculum and standards—are functions of the "political economy of truth" and of the "constant economic and political incitement" that truth is subject to (p. 131). Hence, education is one of the apparatuses implicated in the circulating of truths through society, and educational practices are inextricably linked with the political and economic ideologies of the powerful.

As a result, the regime of truth operationalized by the political-economic-institutional structure that functions in education very effectively oppresses those most intimately involved yet least empowered in teaching and learning—namely students and teachers—and prohibits them from becoming emancipated from, or even recognizing, its oppressive network. Yet, according to Foucault (2000), the key to changing the locus of power does not necessarily exist in "emancipating truth from every system of power... but in detaching the power of truth from the forms of hegemony, social, economic and cultural, within which it operates" (p. 133). This is the potent power of critical pedagogy: to release students and educators from the hegemonic practices in education through illuminating taken-for-granted assumptions and discovering the means to produce new truths or paradigm shifts. This potential power also represents an area of criticism from both inside and outside of critical pedagogical thought and practices, in that new truths, even those that emerge from resistance to oppressive power, have the potential to create new exclusionary practices. In Foucault's construct, the reverse of power is resistance, not powerlessness. Further, power and resistance are interrelated and coexist; neither can exist without the other. Hence, the resistance itself may operate within hegemonic principles, and may create new oppressive forms of power. Freire (1970) emphasized that it is incumbent upon critical practitioners and their students to ensure that questions related to power and resistance are reflected upon with, not on behalf of or in a way that imposes such reflection upon those who would be educated, and this is indeed a caution that must be taken most seriously:

> *O grande problema está em como poderão os oprimidos, que "hospedam" ao opressor em si, participar da elaboração, como seres duplos, inautênticos, da pedagogia de sua libertaçao. Somente na medida em que se descubram "hospedeiros" do opressor poderão contribuir para o partejamento de sua pedagogia libertadora.* (p. 17)

> The great problem is in how the oppressed, who have "hosted" in themselves the oppressor, as dual, inauthentic beings, are able to participate in the development of the pedagogy of their liberation. Only to the degree to which they discover themselves as "hosts" of the oppressor can they contribute to the midwifery of their liberating pedagogy.

Therefore, it is not sufficient to engage in resistance to power without recognizing that liberation itself begs such questions as: "liberation from what or whom?"; "to what end or purpose?"; "how does or has the nature of oppression, the oppressed, or the oppressor changed in liberation?"; and, "what is the nature of the resistance from some other source that emerges in liberation?" Critical pedagogy relies on a cycle of reflection, conscientization and action, as described by Freire (1970), and this cycle maintains the component of awareness that, ideally, would constantly refresh the liberatory spirit and keep the work of liberation honest and of the moment.

Forsan et haec olim meminisse iuvabit

Critical pedagogy is grounded in a tradition of thought that can be traced, at least in the West, to ancient Greece[5] and (like its progenitor, critical theory) is rooted in the belief in the emancipatory capacity of knowledge, in the potential for critical discourse and language to open social systems and individuals to new paths that expose oppression and seek to create alternative systems and ways of being that liberate individuals and society (Freire, 1970; Guilherme, 2002; Leonardo, 2004; Luke, 2004). Giroux, McLaren, and others (Darder, Baltodano, & Torres, 2003; Guilherme, 2002) have linked John Dewey with the initial impulse in the United States toward educational practices that centered on active student engagement in learning and the processes of democracy in education (Dewey, 2004), creating a "language of possibility" which Giroux (1988) asserts was fundamental for the establishment of critical thought in education. However, there have been other educational movements and activists whose ideas were prototypical of critical educational theory, particularly in the naming of oppression, dominance and the possibility of resistance by the oppressed. Some of the most strident criticism of the racist and classist practices perpetrated in education in the United States during the nineteenth and early twentieth centuries came from African American scholars and activists. W. E. B. Du Bois (1961), for example, issued harsh invectives against the subjugation of African Americans by white liberals and conservatives alike, and against the pandering of Booker T. Washington to the dominant White society and his resultant neglect of a truly revolutionary or liberating approach to African American education. When the dust of the Civil War had settled, what had remained for Black society in the post-Civil War era were more vigorous and vicious racism, harsher economic conditions, and increasing alienation from power. At the beginning of the twentieth century, the spirit of dissent and revolution had been articulated and inspired, in part, by Du Bois. As he famously stated, "Three centuries' thought has been the raising and unveiling of [the] bowed human heart, and now behold a century new for the duty and the deed. The problem of the Twentieth Century is the problem of the color-line" (p. 29). Du Bois focused much of his work on the fact that, in the United States, racism and the economy were intertwined, and viewed the reticence on the part of African Americans like Washington to rock the White-dominated social boat by subduing the pursuit of true equity and equality as a viable path as the entrenchment of an

American apartheid (a term Du Bois would not have known, but which he would have understood all too well). He also proposed that aspects of Marxism and socialism provided an antidote for the burden of capitalism's chokehold on the poor and vulnerable (Du Bois, 2005), a view that later educational philosophers and theorists (e.g., McLaren and Giroux) would use as elements of a foundation for resistance to the institutionalized oppression that characterizes capitalism. When we consider Du Bois's (1961) statement that "The black men of America have a duty to perform, a duty stern and delicate.... By every civilized and peaceful method we must strive for the rights which the world accords to men" (pp. 38-39), we recognize similar exhortations in Freire and other modern critical pedagogues; in it, we may also hear echoes of Socrates in the *Apology* (29 c-d), when he asserted that people have not only the right, but a duty to resist the state if it should interfere with their right to question the state.

Apple, Au, and Gandin (2009b) describe a history of critical education that traces the movements in education that arose organically from the struggles of those who faced oppression on a number of fronts. Organizations emerged in the United States that challenged oppressive practices in education and sought new paths for addressing inequities and conditions that were counter to the espoused beliefs in freedom and equality. For example, early teachers' unions were born in the early 1900s from women's mobilizations against oppressive male-dominated practices and unfair pay structures in education and provided the foundation for challenging dominance in class and gender relations. Community groups, such as the Harlem Community for Better Schools, an interracial coalition of African American parents, Jewish socialist and communist teachers, and church and community groups that had as their mission the improvement of education in their community in the 1930s to 1950s, and Socialist Sunday Schools in the early 1900s, emerged as grassroots efforts that provided an empowered resistance to oppressive forces and unfair practices in race and class dynamics in education (Apple, Au, & Gandin, 2009b, pp. 5-6). These groups are important to note because they represented the critical activism "at its best," because they sought the involvement of stakeholders in education (students, parents, teachers and community members) in ways that the "professional learning communities" of today's schools can only hope to emulate.

The Social Reconstructionists in the United States, among them Harold Rugg (1886-1960), George Counts (1889-1974), and Theodore Brameld (1904-1987), represented a small group of educators associated with the progressive philosophy who put forth the idea that education was not only crucial to and for the purposes of participation in a democratic society; rather, it was also an instrument for the perpetuation of dominance and subjugation in society, and as a center of cultural politics, it must also be the center for engendering the empowerment of the educated (Giroux, 2005). They wrote about the social obligations of educators, and particularly cautioned against educational policies that demonstrated the increasing involvement and influence of politics and the market in public education. In many ways, the words of the Reconstructionists resonate with those of the critical pedagogues of the late twentieth and early twenty-first centuries. George Counts (1932), in his essay titled, "Dare Progressive Education be Progressive?" maintained that while progressive educators (which included Counts' colleague John Dewey) had emphasized placing the interests and growth of the child at the center of education, with activity related to life situations as the educational focus, it had not gone far enough; it "[brought] into the picture but one half of the landscape." He made the following statement, which sounds particularly contemporary: "The need for the founding of Progressive Education on an adequate social theory is peculiarly imperative today. We live in troublous times; we live in an age of profound change; we live in an age of revolution" (p. 31). For today's critical theorists, this is a familiar call to action.

The concern of the Reconstructionists was for the advancement of a social theory that would activate the citizenry to consider the most challenging issues relating to social justice during the turbulent first half of the twentieth century. As "Progressive" as progressive educators thought that education could be, Counts (1922) and other Reconstructionists believed there were serious and potentially dangerous gaps:

> The great weakness of Progressive Education lies in the fact that it has elaborated no theory of social welfare, unless it be that of anarchy or extreme individualism. In this, of course, it is but reflecting the viewpoint of the members of the liberal-minded upper middle class who provide most of the children for the Progressive school.... [A]t heart feeling themselves members of a superior breed, they do not want their children to mix too freely with children of the poor or of the less fortunate races. Nor do they want them to accept radical social doctrines or espouse unpopular causes. According to their views, education should deal with life, but with life at a distance or in a highly diluted form. Indeed they would generally maintain that life should be kept at arm's length. (pp. 7-9)

The Reconstructionists, like modern critical pedagogues, recognized that at the heart of the social injustices in America was class and identity struggle, the concept of "Other-ness" experienced by oppressed or alienated people, and the overwhelming pressure of capitalism on social and political structures.

Counts' statement that "any concrete school program will contribute to the struggle that is ever going on among institutions, ideas and values; it cannot remain neutral in any firm and complete sense" (as cited in Gutek,

2006, p. 16) is strongly reflected in the views of such critical pedagogues as McLaren and Giroux. His assertion that education is contextualized, "a product of its time, place and circumstance" (p. 19) recalls similar contentions of Foucault, whose genealogy conceptualized the historicity of knowledge, truth and power, and of Paulo Freire (1970), who emphasized that education must be situationally based:

> *É na realidade mediatizadora, na consciência dela tenhamos educadores e povo, que iremos buscar o conteúdo programático da educação.* (p. 49)

> It is in the mediating reality, in the awareness that educators and the people have of that, to which we must go to find the programmatic content of education.

McLaren and Giroux's pronouncements regarding the deleterious effects of the dominant discourses of economics in society recall several of Counts' (1932) claims:

> The achievement of this goal [to usher in an age of plenty, to make secure the lives of all, and to banish poverty forever from the land] would require fundamental changes in the economic system. Historic capitalism, with its deification of the principle of selfishness, its reliance upon the forces of competition, its placing of property above human rights, and its exaltation of the profit motive, will either have to be displaced altogether, or so radically changed in form and spirit that its identity will be completely lost. (pp. 46-47).

For as long as economic disparity and imbalance of power has existed among sectors of the population in societies, there have been powerful expressions of the dichotomies that emerge. Freire described the problem as, in part, one of the mindset of the powerful (the "oppressors"):

> *O dinheiro é a medidi de todas as coisas.... Ter mais ... é um privilegio desumanizante.... Direito que "conquistaram com seu esforça, com sua coragem de correr risco".... Se os outros—" esses invejosos"—não têm, é porque são incapazes e preguiçosos, a que juntam ainda um injustificável mal-agradecimento a seus "gestos generosos." E, porque "mal-agradecidas e invejosos," são sempre vistas os oprimidos com seus inimigos potenciais a quem têm de observar e vigiar.* (pp. 25-26)

> Money is the measure of all things.... To have more is a dehumanizing privilege, a right that "they won with their effort, with their courage to run risks...." If the others—"those envious ones"—do not "have," it is because they are incapable and lazy, with which they combine an unjustifiable ingratitude toward their "generous gestures." And, because they are "ungrateful and envious," the oppressed are always viewed as their potential enemies whom they have to watch and monitor.

George Counts (2004) wrote the following in 1932, referring to a conflict that reached back to early American history, between the Jeffersonian ideal of a democratic and egalitarian state that embraced human rights and liberty and Hamiltonian focus on economics, a ruling elite and private special interests (also discussed in Gutek, 2006), which he saw as the root of social problems during the Great Depression:

> The hypocrisy which is so characteristic of our public life today is due primarily to our failure to acknowledge the fairly obvious fact that America is the scene of an irreconcilable conflict between two opposing forces. On the one side is the democratic tradition inherited from the past; on the other is a system of economic arrangements which increasingly partakes of the nature of industrial feudalism. (pp. 34-35)

While Counts vigorously decried the influence of "industrial feudalism" on schooling, Harold Rugg (1921) wrote about the neglect of curricular focus in social studies to inform students about the "development of current institutions and problems," which ought to have been "the avowed purpose of public school instruction in history" (p. 45). Rugg proposed that the social studies curriculum be focused on those topics that held the greatest social value for a "troubled society" (Rugg, as cited in Evans, 2007, p. 42), and that students must be educated to acquire awareness of the problems of society so that they would become actively engaged in the improvement of those problems. In the topics he proposed for the reconstructed curriculum, he took on the problematization of the market, labor relations, control and centralization of industry, and "the story of 'how America developed agencies' for the development of public opinion" and "the history of experiments in government so ... as to give a critique of the relative fitness of various forms of government with which society has experimented to secure adequate expression of either popular opinion or most intelligent opinion" (p. 47). Rugg was vilified by educators and politicians in the 1930s and 1940s who found his textbook reform requirements too radical, too potentially subversive. Several national organizations, including the Advertising Federation of America, the National Association of Manufacturers, and in particular that bastion of fundamentalist nationalism, the American Legion, went on a vigorous offensive against Rugg's junior and senior high school textbooks, in which he had ostensibly portrayed advertising and industry in a critical light. Eventually, Rugg was accused of being a Communist, sales of his textbooks plummeted, and some school districts banned his textbooks. As Evans points out, in the context of the Great Depression, Rugg's attempt to encourage students to critically examine social problems and to commit to social activism was interpreted as a threat in the midst of rising paranoia about the security of America's industrial and political interests, at home and abroad (Riley, 2006).

The Progressives and the Social Reconstructionists in education represented, in many ways, the revolutionary voice of the first half of the twentieth century, using "the language of possibility" as a response to the economic, political and philosophical crises in the United States and the world. "The 1930's were not small times," as Ponder (2006) euphemistically reminds us, and as enrollments in public education began to swell and students were increasingly educated through high school, the potential for social reform and a new public consciousness appeared to exist within the walls of schools. Social reconstruction in education offered one of the most critical looks at society and its mechanisms in the United States since the Civil War. As Watkins (2006) points out, the Reconstructionists "took up highly volatile and super-charged political issues of power, property, wealth distribution, knowledge selection, and societal reform as few other groups of educators, before or after, have dared" (p. 211). Although critical pedagogues have rather inconsistently traced their lineage to the Reconstructionists,[6] it is clear that they share many common themes in their work.

Modern critical educational theorists trace the greatest influence on the development of critical pedagogy to the members of the Frankfurt School. Founded initially in response to the limitations of Marxism and its focus on labor in the face of an increasingly oppressive capitalism in the West, and the lack of resistance by the populations under the thumb of dictatorial regimes in Europe (Held, 1980; Jay, 1996), the Frankfurt School focused on critical views of the hegemonic practices (spawned by political and economic forces) that perpetuated injustices in education and society. Among the most central arguments of the Frankfurt School were its criticisms of positivism's hijacking of reason in the modern West in the twentieth century and its advocacy of reliance upon science, specifically the scientific method, as the dominating force in knowledge generation (McLaren, 2003). Giroux (2003a) uses a quote by Friedman, to explain the problem: "Reason, under the rule of positivism, stands in awe of the fact.... Its task ends when it has affirmed and explicated the fact.... Under the rule of positivism, reason inevitably stops short of critique" (p. 32). In its association of positivism with political conservatism and ideological hegemony, the Frankfurt School moved critical theory into a contrast with the positivist legacy of "value neutrality" (p. 35), a legacy we find prominently underpinning recent educational reforms since the passage of the No Child Left Behind Act.[7] By eliminating the availability of critical examination through an overemphasis on positivist valuations, we become like Plato's prisoners in the cave (Republic, VII), chained to the wall in the dark, unaware that our reality, which consists only of shadows from the outside world that are produced by firelight, is merely a projection, a phantom of a much more complex existence beyond that which we take as truth. As such, we rely exclusively on what we believe are the "facts," of what is empirically observable or upon scientific knowledge, for our conception of reality, thereby obviating the possibility for ethical or critical considerations.

This critique opened the door to those adherents of the Frankfurt School who would later develop further critical theory, which viewed "what is" or what is thought to be, from the lens of what other possibilities could exist; that is, rather than accepting as fact that which is verifiable by virtue of the senses. The critical theorists of the Frankfurt School viewed the development of "consciousness"—of an "inward awareness"—as the path beyond reason or scientific knowledge toward emancipation.

To see "fact" through an historical-cultural lens, it is possible to see how what we come to know is constructed through complex, elaborate systems of relationships and interplay between power, knowledge, and an historically-constructed present. The work of Adorno, Horkheimer, and Marcuse, which Henry Giroux (2003a) and others have described (Held, 1980; Jay, 1996), resonates strongly with Foucault's descriptions of power-knowledge structures and the relational bases for truths.[8] Giroux also discusses the shortcomings of the Frankfurt School adherents' insights, particularly in the realm of practical application. For example, while the critical theory proposed by these theorists provided a framework from which to view the presence and impact of positivism in education, the work itself offers little in the way of practical application toward a theory of radical pedagogy. As Giroux points out, these theorists "underestimated the radical potential inherent in working-class culture," and hence they "developed an unsatisfactory notion of dominance" and "never explored the contradictory modes of thinking that characterize the way most people view the world" (p. 55). These are serious shortcomings, indeed, particularly if we are to envision a mode of pedagogy that assumes a potential for liberation in education through transformation of accepted roles and norms in systems of domination. Still, as Giroux argues, within the contributions of the Frankfurt School, we have the beginnings of a framework for examining and "reformulating" the contributions of critical theory in the construction of pedagogy that considers both historical conditions and the capacity for liberation.

The Frankfurt School thinkers paved the way for various philosophies of critical educational practices, several of which are explored below. Giroux, in his essay on critical theory and practice (in Darder et al., 2003) discusses the contributions that the Frankfurt School's insights made to the development of critical pedagogy, including their critique of positivist rationality, their view of critical theory in opposition to traditional theory (p. 55) that its proponents suggested, and the ways of critically reconstructing culture. Because ideologies are shaped by or are products of the dominant culture, even in the most benign educational systems (whether in classroom, schools, districts, states or nations) that have not engaged in critical self-examination in effect engage in further destruction through various types of neglect, or more violent forms of denial. For example, despite the rhetoric of the recent political-economic-institutional regime in the United States to "leave no child behind," the degree of neglect of the nondominant culture by those in power has been devastating. Neglect or denial of individual's capacity to act against various types of oppression, neglect, or denial of the physical and social environments that are supposed to support humanity, and neglect or denial of the development of a self-consciousness centered on self-care and care of others, has resulted in the destruction of opportunities for students and teachers to be free from subjugation in their present situations, for them to become more compassionate, and ultimately more engaged with seeking peaceful, cooperative relationships with all systems that make up life on earth. The critical pedagogy theories and practices described below offer hope for the reversal of such neglect and renewal of positive possibilities for education.

Audentis Fortuna iuvat

The importance of Paulo Freire to the development of critical pedagogy in North America cannot be overstated, and most critical pedagogy theorists credit him as essentially the "inaugural philosopher of critical pedagogy" (McLaren, 1999, p. 49). Leonardo (2004) asserted that "pedagogy first became critical with Freire," and that Freire "gave education a language that neglected neither the effect of oppression on concrete people nor their ability to intervene on their behalf" (p. 12). Glass (2001), joining Giroux, McLaren and others in citing the injurious effects of capitalist maneuverings in a global economy, and political justifications of policies that have served to create increasingly dangerous imbalances in power in society, declared that "a pedagogy of the oppressed is as needed today as when Freire first articulated it" (p. 15). In ways that perhaps no other critical educator has done, Freire (1970) lived his philosophy, having been shaped by his experiences in the dire circumstances of his early life and in his work with peasants in Brazil. Many critical pedagogues who have described their personal impressions of Freire mention the impact of his presence as their friend and mentor, and the love that he inspired and that he invoked in his public speeches and personal interactions with students and colleagues. His idea of teaching as "an act of love" was a concept he lived, a fierce brand of love that opposed the "insipid 'generosity' of teachers and administrators" who perpetuate systems of dominance and oppression in society, and which, as a radical, political form of love, was rooted in joining others in the struggle to become more fully "human" (Darder, 2003). For Wink (2005), he was "the quintessential teacher and learner" (p. 83), who worked to erase the dichotomous boundaries between these two roles by engaging himself and others in examining the education as politics, and the "educability" of the politics (Shor & Freire, 2003).

Freire (1970) sought to reclaim education as liberation for those whose benefit it ought to have been conceived: those involved in the processes of teaching and learning. He occupies a space in education that is both a crossroads and a starting point between the ancient (Western) world of Socrates, with critical reflection as a path to freedom of the mind and improvement of the self, and modern-day critical pedagogy with its emphasis on critical reflection toward action for the liberation of society as well as individuals. According to Freire, such liberation becomes possible when we discard the "banking processes" of education that perpetuate systems of domination and oppression, in which students are merely receptacles for the "deposits" of information handed down to them from teachers. Dialectic processes, which require the breaking down of the normative roles of teacher and student and the re-forming of those relationships into teacher-as-student, student-as-teacher, transform education from a traditional "banking" model to a "problem-posing" model, with students as "*investigadores críticos em diálogo com o educador, investigador critico, também,*" critical investigators in dialogue with the teacher, also a critical investigator (pp. 39-40). Through dialogue, and a level field of relationships, teachers and students become conscious of systems of power/knowledge, and it is that conscientization (*conscientizacao*), that creates the foundation for change. In dialetical praxis, the participatory aspects of dialogue, the quality of the questions, an interaction between theory and practice, the willingness to become curious and reflective about one's position in the world, a respect for the knowledge of learners (and one's own learning, as a teacher), and a commitment to "*da ética universal do ser humano.... A ética ... afrontada na manifestação discriminatória de raça, de gênero, de classe,*" a universal human ethic that is affronted by racial, gender and class discrimination (Freire, 1996, p. 7) are essential to transformational teaching and learning that are the hallmarks and goals of critical pedagogy.

Critical theorists in education have frequently pointed out that, in market-driven educational philosophies, the capitalist "spirit of competition" that is so valued in (at least Western) society, and "scientific" measures of acquisition of knowledge and skills have served to turn students and teachers into the objects of education. How can we turn out more students who can make the United States more competitive in the increasingly global marketplace? How can we make teachers more accountable for turning out better students? How can we measure the success of students and teachers so that they achieve the economic and political aims of our government (which are by nature hegemonic)? These are the questions of a society that has built itself upon the discourse of competition, market economy, and capitalism. But these are not the questions that can result in the empowerment of humanity, or that can put humans on the path of freedom from oppression, happiness and equality that our society maintains is the foundation of its collective beliefs. Giroux (2005), quoting Barbara Finkelstein, effectively illustrates the labor-market perspective that has grounded current educational ideology:

> As if they have had enough of political democracy, Americans, for the first time in a one-hundred-and-fifty-year history, seem ready to do ideological surgery on their public schools—cutting them away from the fate of social justice and political democracy completely and grafting them instead onto elite corporate, industrial, military and cultural interests. (p. 17)

Giroux (2003a, 2005) has focused much of his work on the influence of corporate culture and media on democracy and schooling. In particular, he argues that education for citizenship, once central to the educational ideals in the U.S., is under increasing attack by the dominant, conservative, market-oriented discourse that has steered the course of reforms in education since the early twentieth century, but most prominently in the years since the publication of *A Nation at Risk* in 1983. The discourse of such democratic ideals of freedom and justice has been replaced by discourse of a "blatantly more conservative notion of 'patriotism'" (Giroux, 2005, p. 18), and as a result, students in schools are rarely if ever invited or welcomed into discussions or investigations of what "democratic ideals" are really about in the realities and practices of modern Western society; where such discussions could exist, teachers are often constrained by curricular or subject area limitations, if not also by administrative restrictions regarding what is acceptable to say in class. Even more rarely are students (or teachers) afforded the opportunity to engage in "subversive" dialogue, in which they might question the relevance or implications of dominating structures such as standardized testing, for example, or to whom and for whose benefit concerns with "accountability" really apply. As Apple and Beane (2007) assert, " Local decision-making (in schools) is glorified in political rhetoric while federal legislation moves toward national standards, … scripted curriculum, and national tests…. Demands are made to emphasize critical thinking while censorship of school programs and materials increases" (p. 3).

The call for accountability in education exists as part of the evidence of the market's dominance of the public and private lives of citizens. Giroux (2005) draws in part upon the work of Freire as a model for investigating how human experiences are regulated by systems of dominance and subjugation in schools, as schools are institutions that reflect hegemonic practices of society in general. He weaves together the politics of pedagogy and the politics of production in government, media and labor, and urges the further development of critical pedagogy that engages teachers at the front line as social activists, with broad support from other political and social movements that are focused on critical and emancipatory goals.

McLaren (2007) has focused on global issues of oppression and subjugation, as the military-industrial-economic dominance of the United States continues to place the world's most vulnerable populations at risk. He has articulated the goal of his focus in critical pedagogy as opposition to the imperialistic roots of many of the "-isms" that have served to establish the us-them dichotomies that have waged war on the poor, non-dominant classes in the world. With his position firmly set in Marxist humanism, McLaren vigorously castigates the powerful neoconservatives and neoliberals in the United States who, in seeking to perpetuate and expand their power and economic advantages, continue to oppress the indigenous and the poor, the immigrants and the laborers, the teachers and the students in schools.

Ira Shor (1992, 2003), Michael Apple and others articulate other visions of critical educational theory that lend themselves to the advancement of notions of critical pedagogy that broaden its range and reach. Shor, like Freire, has focused on the practice of critical teaching and learning as political acts, with the potential to empower or oppress students and teachers, and in large part his work has concerned education as a means of challenging the status of knowledge and power in schooling and in society. Apple (1995, 2001, 2004, 2009a, 2009b) has written extensively on the relationship between culture, politics and power in the making and enactment of policy and practice in education. For example, he has asserted the presence of four groups, "social forces" unified by ideology, that have influenced the direction of educational policy making in the United States, referred to by Apple as "conservative modernization." These four groups, referred to by Apple (2001) as "neoliberals, neoconservatives, authoritarian populist religious conservatives, and the professional and managerial middle class" (p. 31), have created new "truths," new conceptualizations of and discourses about democracy and citizenship in the twenty-first century, understandings which are often at odds with other discourses of freedom, equity, and justice.

Freire, McLaren, Giroux, and Apple represent a small but important sample of the critical pedagogy theorists who have offered their important ideas to a composite view of critical pedagogy. However, there are theorists and practitioners in the range of critical pedagogies who in fact may not wish to be represented in such a narrow survey of critical ideas.

Critical pedagogy, as defined by these men, but also as a more general concept, has not been without its detractors on the side of liberatory educators. For example, feminist pedagogues (such as Ellsworth, 1989; Gore, 1993, 2003; Lather, 1998, 2001; Luke & Gore, 1992) have argued against the exclusionary nature of critical pedagogy as it is defined and theorized today. Recalling Foucault's model of power and resistance, just as critical pedagogy represents a form of resistance against dominant power, that very resistance evinces a power that is likely to enforce new forms of subjugation, dominance or exclusion. Ellsworth (1989) describes the goals, assumptions, and terminology used and embraced by critical pedagogues as "repressive myths that perpetuate relations of domination" (p. 298), whereby the dictates of critical pedagogy regarding "who" students and teachers "should be" and "what" they "should be doing" appeared to limit or exclude some forms of diversity. Gabel (2002) addresses what she views as some of critical pedagogy's limitations, specifically regarding the lack of consideration of people with diverse abilities. While she allows that critical pedagogy's theoretical commitment to opposing oppression of marginalized persons and groups might assume a de facto inclusion of those traditionally referred to as "disabled," she also views the complete absence of the viewpoints and struggles of people of diverse abilities (or of the disabled) in the most foundational literature (in particular, Freire, Giroux, and McLaren) as a conceptual problem of critical pedagogy. Pointing out Freire's notion of conscientization as relying on "sociocognitive skills" of critique and self-transformation, Gabel asserts that if Freire had considered ability diversity in his construct, he might have also considered that, because disability is a form of oppression imposed from outside, a social construct, and not an inherently problematic condition with which those with diverse abilities always self-identify as "disability," he might also have considered that "non-disabled people are the ones who need to change" (pp. 186-187). She also takes McLaren (1998) to task in his use of "disabled" in an article (p. 431)[9] in which he refers to an inertia and lack of capacity on the part of the "Marxist educational Left" to effect change. In blaming the Left for its lack of fortitude by using the language of disability in this context, McLaren has ventured into what Reagan (2002b) has referred to as an "etic" construct, in this case, of disability, a deficit construct that may come dangerously close to oppressive enactments. This understanding of ability diversity or disability as "deficit" is evident, according to Gabel and other scholars, in many discourses in pedagogy, including those that are considered to be critical or liberatory pedagogies. Gabel contends that "the ways we use terms and understand people's experiences in theory have significant consequences for the enactment of theory into practice" (p. 186).[10] In attempting to engage in a critical pedagogy, we cannot afford to use terminology or any words indiscriminately. Freire (1970) himself reminds us that the essence of the dialogue he espoused as the *"conquista do mundo para a libertação do homens,"* or the "conquering of the world for the liberation of human beings" (p. 39) is the word (*palavra*). The word is our route to human existence and the means to "transform the world (*transformar o mundo*)," (p. 41). As such, he cautions, *"ninguém pode dizer a palavra verdadeira sozinho, ou dizê-la para os outros, num ato de prescrição, com o qual rouba a palavra aos demais;* [No one is able to say a true word, or to say it on behalf of some other, an act of prescription with which s/he steals it from another]" (p. 41).

Gore (2003) challenges the politics of empowerment in critical pedagogy, wherein the teacher as empowered agent who seeks to empower some Other, thus establishing a problematic "us/them" distinction. With so much theorizing and publishing in critical pedagogy taking place in the Academy, it is difficult not to consider the potential danger Gore warns against, which is "apparent both in the work of the teacher who is to empower students, and in the work of the academic whose discourse is purportedly empowering for the teachers (and others)." "Arrogance" Gore explains, "can underlie claims of 'what we can do for you'" (p. 338). She also criticizes Giroux, in his assertion that teachers are intellectuals who cannot deceive themselves regarding their complicity in perpetuating Foucauldian "regimes of truth," for failing to recognize his own contradictory position as an academic intellectual in functioning also within regimes of truth. Further, Gore suggests that radical pedagogies, including the critical pedagogy of Giroux and McLaren, may face legitimate criticisms for being "U.S.-centric discourses," as many of the questions raised by critical pedagogy focus on issues related to practices in North America. At the very least, it is possible to consider the "historical, material, and social conditions that contribute to the construction of radical pedagogies" (p. 46), and the assumptions that follow from these constructions warrant a reflexivity that is sometimes, perhaps often, absent in the theorizing of critical pedagogues (De Lissovoy, 2003; Worth, 1993).

While there can be little dispute that critical pedagogy theories have contributed to a vibrant conversation in the academy that has raised the consciousness of some educators on the front lines in public schools, it may also be observed that critical pedagogy has not had as much presence in the arena of public educational reform and policy change as might be hoped for by those who seek a turn toward truly liberatory education. In fact, the reality appears to be that today, in the era of "accountability-as-reform" that has defined at least the last decade, in which the surveillances of high-stakes testing and No Child Left Behind's broad effect on every facet of education have served to regulate the time and space of teaching and learning, policies have tended to limit opportunities for a praxis of critical education. Multicultural education is one aspect of a potentially critical pedagogy that has received much press, print, and lip service, but appears to have had relatively little or consistent impact on practices, beyond so-called "diversity training" professional development programs for teachers, "multi-cultural celebrations," and "tolerance" seminars for adults and students (Kubota & Austin, 2007; Nieto, 1999). In the United States, the dogged pursuit of a cultural unity has emphasized a monocultural viewpoint; the discourses of unity itself, long part of a national ethos that reflects how America has defined becoming "one out of many," have taken on increasingly protectionist or imperialist tones, and, more insidiously, "Otherization" from the Sputnik era forward, having reached their low point following the events of 9/11.

Ne credite equo

One area in which American monoculturism has had its most significant impact is in the area of foreign language education. At the same time that there have been now several centuries of education in foreign languages in the United States, policies and practices in second-language teaching and learning have largely, though perhaps not explicitly, promoted monolingualism, with language planning policies and implementations that have virtually ensured that few if any foreign language students in the U.S. will ever achieve meaningful proficiency in a language other than American English. Reagan and Osborn (2002) have raised important points regarding the political aspects of language planning, particularly regarding the political nature of policy:

> In fact, language policies and related language planning decisions are frequently made solely or primarily on the basis of short-term political expediency, misguided assumptions and beliefs, and a range of extralinguistic factors. It is also true, however, that language policies and language planning activities are quite often unsuccessful (sometimes spectacularly so), often precisely because of the way in which they were designed and implemented. (p. 114)

It is important to note that, as Canagarajah (2005b) has pointed out in the case of second language (specifically, in his studies, English language), learning, critical pedagogy had little or no presence in the theory and methodological discourse in second language teaching and learning until the late 1980s to 1990s (p. 931). Because second language education in English had served for centuries to maintain, through the inherently hegemonic force of teaching the language of a dominating, colonizing, majority culture to so-called minority-language students, teachers had adopted "an idyllic innocence," supported by structuralist and positivist philosophies and pedagogical approaches that had maintained a strong hold in education through the late twentieth century. Those presumably apolitical approaches, including behavioralist models of training students, methods grounded in "scientifically-based" practices that could produce student learning through "neutral" and "objective" student-teacher experiences, and a "value-free" grounding in grammar instruction obscured the potentially dangerous reality of what second language teaching and learning was really about, and a relative blindness to the political and hegemonic presence in second language education persisted longer than it had in education's counterparts in literacy (see Canagarajah, 2005a, 2005b).

Contributing to the absence of a critical grounding in language education is the fact that there are essentially different visions and versions in language education in the United States that fall along lines of who is being educated, and to what purposes. Labels abound in language education that demonstrate the persistent dichotomies that have served to further separate and "Otherize" learners. There is second language, or L2, education, English as a Second Language (ESL), Engish as a Foreign Language (EFL), Teachers of English to Speakers of Other Languages (TESOL), Languages Other Than English (LOTEs), Limited English Proficiency (LEP) students, and English Language Learners (ELLs). There is also "mainstream" foreign language, or the increasingly common label, "world language education." The labels "second" and "other" emphasize the priority of English in language education, and make potentially dangerous political statements because, at the very least, they trivialize or obscure the assignment of relative values to languages. There is an emerging discomfort with those labels, as educators seek for less-politically charged or more inclusive terminology, as noted in the recently more acceptable "ELL" label to replace "LEP" and "world language" to replace "foreign language" in education (Kubota & Austin, 2007; Osborn, 2000). The attempt to affix more politically correct names on practices that are inherently problematic tends to obfuscate, rather than address, the issues they raise, and Reagan and Osborn (2002) state that the problem is that replacing "nomenclature ... addresses such concerns ... only at the level of *articulated bias*" (p. 8, emphasis in original). Apple (2004) is strident in his admonition that the use of certain language and labels functions as a "form of social control, a 'worthy' successor to that long line of mechanisms in schools that sought to homogenize social reality" (p. 120).

Further, in foreign language education, there has not been extensive action in policy or practice given to critical approaches in mainstream foreign language teaching. Reagan and Osborn (2002) contend that, due to the nature of the intersections of politics, policies, and purposes in foreign language education in the United States, the system, in effect, sets the learner up for a largely unsuccessful language learning experience. Against a backdrop of an educational system with "better things to do" with teaching and learning time because of the demands that standardized testing has placed on the use of that time, and in a society in which the definition of an "educated person" continues to shift attention toward the marketable skills one has acquired through education, the foreign language educator struggles against the marginalization of her subject and her craft. As Kramsch (2000) points out, "What makes foreign language study unique among the subjects taught is that its object or purpose is itself located outside of the American cultural norm" (pp. 321-322). Institutional biases continue to push foreign language to the sidelines of the core content of education, where attention to study and competitiveness in math and science trumps language study and cultural understanding in the global arena (Kubota & Austin, 2007; Reagan & Osborn, 2002). Notions about the "utility" of foreign language learning continue to determine the relative value of languages taught; it is increasingly common for public schools, particularly in difficult economic times, to view foreign language programs with few or decreasing numbers of students[11] as dispensable (Watzke, 2003). In spite of an ongoing Eurocentric bias in foreign language offerings, school districts have recently begun to replace traditionally-taught languages with low enrollments (such as French, German, or Latin) with languages viewed as more economically expedient, or important to ensuring national security and competitiveness in the world, such as Mandarin Chinese and Arabic (Pavlenko, 2003; Sehlaoui, 2008). It remains to be seen whether pedagogy in non-Western languages will be effective or meaningful for students, since local school districts' commitments to resources, primarily to teachers of these languages, and particularly to those from foreign nations, such as China, have tended to be short-lived (even subject to the duration of those teachers' visas), and may be lacking in the pedagogical support these teachers likely need (Manzo, 2006; Yong, 2007). Similarly, it is unlikely that, given the emphasis on utility of foreign language education vis-à-vis competitive capacity, the commitment to teaching and learning non-Western languages will remain strong in the face of the economic reality of what supporting the teachers and students of these languages will actually entail. In short, there may be no long-term rationale or commitment in most public secondary schools for offering Chinese and other "mission-critical" languages at the secondary level in a broad-based fashion as long as there is the perception in the United States that the rest of the world has already committed to and benefitted from learning English (Demont-Heinrich, 2008).

Yet, there is a growing consideration in the United States for teaching foreign languages as a means of developing cultural interactions and understandings, particularly in the interest of increasing awareness and appreciation of diversity and cultural sensitivity in the preparation of students for a "global society."[12] What exactly this means in practice in foreign language education in this regard is not yet clear, although strong positions have been stated, through the American Council of Foreign Language Teachers (ACTFL) and the National Standards in Foreign Language Education Project's document, *Standards for Foreign Language Learning: Preparing for the 21st Century* (2006). This document attempts to define a broad understanding of language learning, in a way that begins to approach what Osborn (2000) refers to as a movement from "words to worlds," a "macrocontextualization" that represents an exploration of the "political, economic, and cultural factors relating to linguistic diversity [that] develop students' skills in understanding the role language that plays in society" (p. 114).

While the revised standards document points to an evolution in language instruction, language educators continue to struggle to help their students making meaning, both literally and more broadly, from the content they learn and the context in which they learn the target language. The artificiality of the context and cultural biases of foreign language education in the United States is enhanced by the content of many language textbooks (e.g., see Herman, 2007, for a discussion of Spanish language textbooks, and Shardakova & Pavlenko, 2004, for a critical review of beginning Russian textbooks used in the United States).[13] Left unquestioned, without being "problematized" from a Foucauldian or critical perspective, learning about cultural "practices and products" in the foreign language classroom is doomed to be scripted by stereotypical "knowledge" (Reagan & Osborn, 2002).[14]

The exploration of culture and communication through foreign language study ought to open doors to the critical (Guilherme, 2002; Osborn, 2006; Reagan & Osborn, 2002), but beyond ESL/TESOL, there has not yet been a strong movement to establish critical pedagogy (or any of the postmodern pedagogies mentioned previously) in language education practices in the United States (see Edwards, 2010). One may seriously question whether the foundations and structures currently in place and policies in force in the United States can or do sufficiently support a critical approach, and whether the traditional concepts regarding language studies that are still in use continue to be appropriate or relevant (Osborn, 2006; Pennycook, 2004b; Reagan, 2004). The national and state standards for foreign language education, foreign language teacher education programming, and institutional structures are in several ways at odds with a critical approach (Reagan & Osborn, 2002). For example, the national *Standards for Foreign Language Learning* (2006) has established a composite approach to structuring language learning that includes "the

Five C's" of culture, communication, connections, comparisons, and Communities as content standards, with no hierarchical arrangement among them. Although the Five C's encourage an integration of knowledge and skills across the *Standards*, and imply that learning a foreign language enhances one's ability to enter the global community, as "linguistically and culturally equipped to communicate successfully in a pluralistic American society and abroad" (p. 7) they are also inherently problematic, first and foremost in that they are standards. Standards necessarily imply hegemony by virtue of the perspective they represent, as the document represents primarily what students who have English as their first language should know and be able to do as a result of their foreign language learning experiences. While the "Statement of Philosophy of the Standards" establishes a vision for "a future in which ALL students will develop and maintain proficiency in English and at least one other language, modern or classical" and that "children who come to school from non-English backgrounds should also have opportunities to develop further proficiencies in their first language," the practical application of this philosophy is burdened by its own language. For example, regarding the word "proficiency," what is considered "proficient," who decides how it is understood, defined, or assessed, for whom it is relevant and by whom it is valued are only some questions raised by that word alone. The idea that students from "non-English backgrounds should have opportunities to develop further proficiencies" in their own languages raises issues regarding linguistic legitimacy (Edwards, 2010; Reagan & Osborn, 2002) that are of serious concern from a critical perspective: who ought to determine what "further proficiencies" are appropriate, necessary, and useful for those students in using their first language—are language varieties of native speakers of "target" languages and the like automatically excluded in demonstrations and determinations of "proficiency"?

Despite the opportunities that the *Standards* do present for reflections on the meaning and elements of culture and language, it is still the case that the potential to explore critically the questions raised by the *Standards* is subject to the interpretation of those implementing the *Standards*. Given the way in which standards across the curricula have been interpreted in the United States in recent years, and in light of the inherently positivist approach with which standards and approaches to language learning have typically been designed (see Osborn, 2006; Reagan, 2004), and which their use tends to promote, it appears unlikely that they will be used in any way other than as a technicist approach to "fixing" language education. Osborn asserts that it is possible to use the *Standards* in a critical approach to foreign language teaching, but also acknowledges the difficulties in the current system that may preclude such an approach. He sees teacher preparation as the foundation for establishing a pedagogy that would open the door to change through using, rather than in spite of, the topics addressed in the *Standards* (p. 44). This suggestion points to other aspects of institutional practices and policies that are in need of broad and deep transformation to support a critical pedagogy in foreign language teaching and learning, a transformation that is at the heart of the remaining chapters of this study.

NOTES

1. Plato, *Theatetus*, in Plato VII: *Theatetus, Sophist (Loeb Classical Library)* in Fowler, H. N. (Trans.) (1921): Cambridge, MA: Harvard University Press.
2. Of course, this view of life is not at all exclusive to the ancient Greeks, nor to Western culture. Buddhism, for example, was founded primarily upon the Buddha's realizations regarding the nature of suffering, which arises from ignorance and lack of "clear seeing." There are almost innumerable sources for and commentaries on the Buddha's teachings, but one of the most accessible for laypeople is the *Dhammapada*, translated by G. Fronsdal (2005).
3. The "Socrates" referred to throughout this dissertation is the one we meet in Plato's writings, since it is through Plato's dialogues that we can acquire the most extensive impression of Socrates and Socratic dialogue. It must be stated, however, that we can augment our ideas about Socrates through the work of Xenophon, Aristotle, and Aristophanes.
4. Several authors make an explicit or implicit distinction between education and schooling, which is particularly instructive for the discussion of the problems posed by critical educators regarding the use of schooling as a means of enculturating and perpetuating imbalances of power in society, as a means of "domesticating" oppression, to use Freire's term (see Darder, 2003; Freire, 1994; Giroux, 2003b, 2005; Kanpol, 1993, 1998; Kincheloe, 2008). Keith Hoskin (in Ball, 1990) traces a similar path for education through the etymology of the word *disciplina* as a combination of *disci-*, meaning "learning" and *"plina"* as a contraction of *"-pulina"* relating to "the child." Hence, Hoskin points out, "discipline" is a means of getting learning into the child.
5. To Socrates, and later to Plato, Aristotle, and others.
6. Giroux (2005, p. 11, and in the endnotes, p. 220) mentions that, although the Reconstructionists represented some of the most radical attempts by educators to critique the interaction of government, education, and citizenship in social formations of power and justice, reconstructionist ideas are virtually absent in contemporary thinking about education, including critical pedagogy. There may be several reasons for this. First, the persecution of the Reconstructionists, particularly Counts, Rugg and Brameld, by the conservatives (with William Randolph Hearst as their propagandist) for their supposed or real Marxist/Communist leanings led to a fairly thorough burial of their ideas and their works, with no resurrection early

enough to make their legacy viable in general considerations of the purposes and goals of education. Second, some critical pedagogues may have
found Counts' retreat from more radical extension of his viewpoints and
his rejection of Marxism to be unsuitable as for their thinking, particularly
as the work of other educationists, such as Freire, provided much more
concrete models for critical pedagogy. Finally, we may take Foucault's concept of the historicity of discourse to understand that reconstructionist
thought may only truly be considered in its context of the 1930s, and that
it was incompatible with the discourses of the Cold War and Sputnik eras.

7. For example, the criteria established by The National Reading Panel
    (National Institute of Child Health and Human Development, 2000) in
    investigating the best methods for teaching reading was the requirement
    that the research used by the panel must meet the gold-standard for exper-
    imental research. Leaving aside the many methodological flaws in the
    Panel's use of research (noted by Panel member Joanne Yatvin and others),
    the fact that the Panel excluded any studies that did not use exclusively
    quantitative methodology automatically excluded the possibility of using
    research done by teachers or other educators using more "subjective" qual-
    itative methodologies.

8. "It is ... not a matter of describing what knowledge is and what power is
    and how one would repress the other ..., but rather, a nexus of knowledge-
    power has to be described so that we can grasp what constitutes the accept-
    ability of a system" (Foucault, 2007, p. 61).

9. Gabel (2002) refers to this quote from McLaren (1998): "The Marxist edu-
    cational Left has, for the most part, carefully ensconced itself within the
    educational establishment in an uneasy alliance that has *disabled* its ability
    to do much more than engage in radical posturing, while reaping the ben-
    efits of scholarly rewards" (emphasis added by Gabel).

10. Reagan (2002b) makes a similar argument in his discussion of "emic" and
    "etic" constructions ("those of participants in the identity" and "those of
    observers outside of," respectively) of Deaf identity. He states that "At
    stake, ultimately, is the question of who defines *deafness*" (p. 45); further, he
    asks us to consider that "if we were to recognize the legitimacy of emic con-
    structions of Deaf identity, the education of deaf children clearly would
    look much different than it does today" (p. 58).

11. Time spent in language instruction also suffers in the era of high stakes
    testing. The report of the Center for Applied Linguistics (Rhodes &
    Pufahl, 2008) found that a third of elementary and secondary schools
    reported that language instruction had been negatively affected by No
    Child Left Behind.

12. Among the themes included in the recent frameworks for "21st century
    learning" developed by the Partnership for 21st Century Skills (2009) is
    "Global Awareness." This is defined in the document as the ability "to
    understand and address global issues," to work collaboratively and to
    respect individuals from diverse cultures and to understand other nations
    and cultures, "including non-English languages."

13. Of course, the U.S. is not alone in its control of what counts as appropriate information in instructional materials. For a critical discussion of Chinese language textbooks used in China and their use in the manipulation of cultural beliefs, see Liu (2005).

14. See also Sercu (2000). The author of this study investigated the degree to which foreign language textbooks contributed to adolescent Flemish students' intercultural competence in learning German language and culture. The investigation focused primarily on cognitive and affective aspects of the development of intercultural competence in students in foreign language classes, in relationship to the content of the textbooks used. Among the conclusions articulated by Sercu is the suggestion that a presentation of cultural information to students in the absence of opportunities to reflect critically on that information may result in students retaining their stereotypical assumptions about the target culture (p. 381).

CHAPTER 4

CIVITAS

National Standards and
the View From Critical Pedagogy

οὐκοῦν, ἦν δ᾽ ἐγώ, ἡ διαλεκτικὴ μέθοδος μόνη ταύτῃ πορεύεται, τὰς
ὑποθέσεις ἀναιροῦσα, ἐπ᾽ αὐτὴν τὴν ἀρχὴν ἵνα βεβαιώσηται, καὶ τῷ ὄντι ἐν
βορβόρῳ βαρβαρικῷ τινι τὸ τῆς ψυχῆς ὄμμα κατορωρυγμένον ἠρέμα ἕλκει
καὶ ἀνάγει ἄνω, συνερίθοις καὶ συμπεριαγωγοῖς χρωμένη αἷς διήλθομεν
τέχναις· ἃς ἐπιστήμας μὲν πολλάκις προσείπομεν διὰ τὸ ἔθος, δέονται δὲ
ὀνόματος ἄλλου, ἐναργεστέρου μὲν ἢ δόξης, ἀμυδροτέρου δὲ ἢ ἐπιστήμης—
διάνοιαν δὲ αὐτὴν ἔν γε τῷ πρόσθεν που ὡρισάμεθα—ἔστι δ᾽, ὡς ἐμοὶ δοκεῖ,
οὐ περὶ ὀνόματος ἀμφισβήτησις, οἷς τοσούτων πέρι σκέψις ὅσων ἡμῖν
πρόκειται.

—Plato (*Republic*, VII, 533c-d)

Therefore, I say, dialectic is the only method that puts aside the
hypotheses in such a manner and takes up the starting point,
grounding itself there, and which, when the eye of the soul is buried
in barbaric muck, gently pulls and leads it upward, using as co-
laborers and assistants in this conversion the skills and arts which we
have often called science through habit, for lack of another name,
clearer than conjecture, more obscure than science—
"understanding," we determined previously. But to me it is not an
argument about the name, but about the great examination that
exists before us.

Consiliō et Animīs: Tracing a Path to Social Justice Through the Classics, pp. 69–95
Copyright © 2012 by Information Age Publishing
All rights of reproduction in any form reserved.

Socrates would not leave unquestioned the reality that evidence or knowledge produced by science appeared to reveal, nor did he trust the assertions of people who claimed to know anything, or the pronouncements about truth from politicians, teachers, or philosophers. Mathematics and sciences that are in modern times and were in Socrates' time often relied upon to measure or explain reality were, in Socrates' reckoning, simply "dreamings about being" ("ονειρωττουσι μεν περι το ον," *Republic. VII.* 533b[1]), and so answers acquired through them were not the substance or the full matter of truth. Rather, according to Socrates, it was dialectic alone that had the power to open a path of inquiry that could bring to light the nature of truth or expose questions that exist underneath commonly held assumptions about reality. The relationship between dialectic and the arts and sciences that Socrates describes here is at the core of a critical perspective. Socrates refers to the sciences as the "assistants" or collaborators in dialectic, not the purveyors of the truth. Dialectic, the hallmark of Socratic dialogue, imposes limitations on the truths assumed by the measurable, the visible, or the self-evident. While it may be folly to declare a something to be true in the absence of evidence that supports that definition, it is perhaps more dangerous to claim or assume, without critically questioning, that evidence or information acquired through scientific or mathematical measurement is neutral, objective, complete in itself and therefore imbued with truth. The danger exists because modernity has deified science and numbers, and thus, thanks to the legacy of the Enlightenment-era equation of science, data and truth, we assume that what matters in education can be measured, and what we are measuring provides meaningful data upon which decisions should be made.[2] Socrates' assertion, that critically questioning that which we think we know or understand to be true from empirical or quantifiable evidence can lift us from the barbaric mire of illusion, is a poignant backdrop for this chapter and for the state of education at this time in the United States, as our nation struggles to understand what is real and what is rhetoric in the debates that rage on about educational reform.

The current preoccupation with standards, measurement, and particularly with quantitative measurement, is both a symptom and a cause of deep insecurity (recalling Ball's [2001] description, of "deep ontological insecurity," referenced earlier, in Chapter 1) in the United States about the quality of public education. Information from national and international standardized assessments, including the National Assessment of Educational Progress (NAEP), the Program for International Student Assessment (PISA), the Trends in International Mathematics and Science Study (TIMMS), and the Progress in International Reading Literacy Study (PIRLS) is used by the U.S. government and others, including corporations and foundations with connections to education, to assess student achievement on a national level. Generally, the data from these sources have been assumed to provide some degree of understanding about where American students are in relation to their international peers in academic knowledge and skills. Politicians, industry leaders and some education experts assert that the data have demonstrated an ongoing inadequacy in student learning in the United States, and this view of the data is widely promulgated through the media. However, there have been a number of other scholars and writers on education who have warned against overinterpretation or misinterpretation of what the data reveal, of the usefulness of the data themselves, and how such measures have been misused to fuel the call for reform, decade after decade (including, among others, Berliner & Biddle, 1995; Bracey, 2004, 2006; Glass, 2008, Meier, 2000; Ravitch, 2010; Rothstein, 1998). They have raised similar concerns regarding the establishment of national standards (created to address the "crisis" in education indicated by testing data), and the creation of standardized tests to go along with the national standards, as the basis for educational assessment and evaluation. Despite the concerns they have raised, it is likely that standards and standardization, as well as curriculum and testing for the purposes of accountability to such standards, will have a firm foothold in education as long as the drive to measure student (and soon, teacher) performance in the manner we have for the past decade continues to have the attention and support of corporate and political power holders.

That the use of data is an important component of acquiring understanding is not in question here. Indeed, critical questioning begins by looking for available data from multiple sources. At issue is the hegemonic use of data: data have been used in the development of rationales for some of the most (or perhaps the most) oppressive policy decisions in the history of public education in the United States. Much of what is made public about data from standardized testing generally and unquestioningly assumes the following: that such examinations or measures are accurate representations of what students should know and be able to do, based on their educational level; that the data from these measures offer appropriate comparisons among comparable groups of students; that these data capture a useful reflection of the status of education in the United States; and that the data contain information that is useful in thinking about how to "reform" education. Of course, there have been many responses to the use of data from these measures that object to the interpretations of what they reveal (Glass, 2008, offers one of the more cogent responses). However, such objections and counterpoints have not had much momentum or effect on public sentiment, nor have they had the wide broadcast necessary to provoke a serious or critical discussion about what we think we know about education, what the most pressing issues are, and how to effectively address them. Unless and until critical dialogue among policymakers and educators is engaged regarding the nature of the data that are used and how they are collected, their purposes, what they can and cannot demonstrate, and how or if they should be used in decision making from the classroom to the policy room, we will continue to reject the voices in our hearts and our heads that continue to prod us ask what is really going on in education in the United States.

Socrates' vision of dialectic—as the only method by which we may pull ourselves out of the quagmire of assumptions and beliefs that have obscured the "eye of our soul"—offers a perspective through which we may examine current discourse about teaching and learning in the United States. Critical questioning is an endeavor that has often been muted by the political purposes that metrics and standardization in education have served in modern times in the United States. In the years since the publication of *A Nation at Risk* (Gardner, 1983), the quest for educational improvement has been fraught with rhetoric and notions of "reform" that warrant critical examination.[3] For at least the last two decades, the national conversation about the condition of education in the United States has been spiked with fear-inspiring, threat-laden buzzwords such as "crisis," "accountability," and "competitiveness." These are dangerously potent words, tightly linked to each other in statements by the media and by politicians, in publications for educators and about education, in policy documents, in the discipline-specific standards documents designed to provide guidance to educators, and in the newly established *Common Core State Standards* (National Governors Association Center for Best Practices and Council of Chief State School Officers, 2010)

Using Foucault and Socrates as "midwives" to assist us in bringing forth critical questions, we may acquire greater understanding of the origin and impact of this discourse on our collective national psyche and may even discover the voice and means by which to resist its effects. Foucauldian concepts, such as governmentality and "technologies of the self" (Foucault, 1988) can help us unveil the discourse that creates (and is created by) the field in which power relationships are established and maintained, and within which the potential for resistance exists. Socratic dialectic encourages us to leave nothing undisturbed ("ἀκινήτους," Republic VII.533c)—assumptions, justifications, declarations, theories or hypotheses must be problematized so that they may be transformed. Foucault described the objective of his work as analyzing the relationships among certain "technologies" humans have employed in understanding and transforming themselves and the world. He described various sciences—including psychiatry, medicine and penology—as "truth games," for the techniques within them that humans have used to discipline and dominate themselves and others. Among the technologies he examined in his work, his chief interests were in the technologies of power, which he said "determine the conduct of individuals and submit them to certain ends or domination," and "technologies of the self," which "permit individuals to effect by their own means or with the help of others a certain number of operations on their own bodies and souls, thoughts, conduct, and way of begin, so as to transform themselves in order to attain a certain state of ...perfection" (Foucault, 1988, p. 18). For example, in the case of the discourse of crisis in education, power is enacted in the ways in which the language of crisis effectively quashes honest debate (indeed, the movement for reform is grounded in an unquestioned certainty that education is in a state of crisis).[4] Therefore, we are compelled to examine the basis of crisis's existence as a belief. The discourse of crisis establishes imbalance in power relationships, and has inevitably led to pronouncements of blame, focused mostly on deficiencies in public education personnel and practices, teachers unions' supposed protection of bad teachers, tenure, and teacher preparation programs. Foucault's methods encourage us to consider the origins of the concept of crisis as an example of "governmentality" where technologies of the self intersect or interact with the technology of power in the domination of others. The discourse of accountability insists on quantifying student performance and teacher effectiveness using measures and purposes that have yet to be meaningfully and critically examined, but which have been used regularly to establish levels of and consequences for "failure." The discourse of competition asserts that there is a global position to be won and maintained, that international dominance in education, as much as in military might and economics, ensures the safety and security of the U.S. and its citizens, and that, were we to lose our competitive edge (mythical though it may be), the consequences would be dire.

The mechanisms of such discourses in education, including the use of standardized tests, publication of scores, state-to-state comparisons, "value-added" and other objective, "scientific" measurements of teacher effectiveness,[5] control of educational structures by noneducators, and standards-based education are the bricks and mortar of education's version of Bentham's *Panopticon*, the prison structure that Foucault (1975) used to symbolize the normalizing and disciplinary features in society. Foucault described the power of the *Panopticon* in this way:

> *De là, l'effet majeur du Panoptique: induire chez le détenu un état conscient et permanent de visibilité qui assure le fonctionnement automatique du pouvoir. Faire que la surveillance soit permanente dans ses effets, meme si elle est discontinue dans son action; ... bref que les détenus soient pris dans une situation de pouvoir dont ils sont eux-mêmes les porteurs.... [L]e pouvoir devait être visible et invérifiable. Visible: sans cesse le détenu aura devant les yeux la haute silhouette de la tour central d'où il est épié. Invérifiable: le détenu ne doit jamais savoir s'il est actuellement regardé; mais il*

doit être sûr qu'il peut toujours l'être.... Le Panoptique est une machine à dissocier le couple voir-être vu: dans l'anneau périphérique, on est totalement vu, sans jamais voir; dans la tour central, on voit tout, sans être jamais vu. (pp. 234-235)

Hence the major effect of the Panopticon: to induce in the prisoner a state of conscious and permanent visibility that assures the automatic functioning of power. To make it so that the surveillance is permanent in its effects, even if it is discontinuous in its action; ... in short, that the prisoners should be taken up in a situation of power of which they are themselves the bearers.... The power should be visible and unverifiable. Visible: the prisoner will unceasingly have before his eyes the tall outline of the central tower from which he is spied upon. Unverifiable: the prisoner must never know if he is actually being watched; but he must be sure that he may always be.... The Panopticon is a machine for dissociating the "to see/to be seen" pairing: in the peripheric ring, one is totally seen, without ever seeing; in the central tower, one sees everything without ever being seen.

Therefore, the mechanisms of discourse about education work to "assure the automatic functioning of power." Like the prisoners in the Panopticon, who learn to sustain the power of the watchtower themselves, educators and students are under constant surveillance from a watchtower built by a political-industrial complex that uses the media to inform a public that has uncritically accepted an increasing corporate influence on educational policy making, virtually since the beginnings of mandatory public schooling in America. In addition, the implicit and explicit assumptions that those mechanisms have established as part of what Gene Glass (2008) has called the "endless narrative of education reform" are that educators have "left children behind" consistently in the last several decades, that teacher unions have been complicit in creating the educational crisis by protecting bad teachers, and that schools' failure to educate our children has put at risk our nation's economic progress.

In a recent statement (February 2010), President Barack Obama expressed the familiar equation of economics, education, and success:

Because economic progress and educational achievement go hand in hand, educating every American student to graduate prepared for college and success in a new work force is a national imperative. Meeting this challenge requires that state standards reflect a level of teaching and learning needed for students to graduate ready for success in college and careers. (Office of the Press Secretary, 2011)

This brief excerpt articulates some of the rhetoric that is the ever-present light in the watchtower that shines on education's prisoners. That rhetoric establishes direct links from political and corporate interests to standards in education, and it asserts the power of standards advocated by government to direct teaching and learning (see, e.g., the National Governors' Association, which was invited by President George H.W. Bush to the first National Summit on Education in 1989, and which established the *Common Core State Standards* initiative in 2009). Further, it defines what the public should believe is the purpose of education: ensuring economic progress. Control from the corporate-political *Panopticon* begins with the assumption that standards are reasonable means by which to establish what must be taught. That assumption provides that standardized assessments are appropriate for measuring who is or is not learning, relying on the notion that current assessments do in fact measure learning related to the standards in some relevant manner. The supposed objectivity of standardized assessment (with its scales that measure failure and ranges of nonfailure) now provide evidence for placing blame on those—inevitably upon schools, and ultimately on the teachers—who are not meeting the educational needs of students.

What is absent from the current rhetoric is just as noteworthy as what is there. For example, there is no mention of the interests of the educated, beyond the reference to success, and it is appears that the success the government seeks for its subjects is limited in measurement to prescribed levels of achievement on standardized tests, graduation from high school, and, most recently, the unquestioned goal of college for all. The purpose of "successful" completion of schooling for all is defined primarily as the production of a population of workers who will grant to the United States an economically competitive edge in the global market. Conservative and corporate reformers of education have advocated school choice and vouchers as a means of spurring competition to enhance education, in the way that the "free market" is supposed to operate, and the voices of corporate reform convinced us that the achievement of the ideals of equity and equality in education is a function of how well students develop into workers who will help the United States to compete in our global society.

There are other types of progress that are rarely, if ever, mentioned in discussions of the global interests of the United States, but which may also be considered as important aspects of educational purpose. For example, there is the development of the compassionate educated person, one educated in the aspects of care as described by Nel Noddings (2005). There is the critically- and socially-conscious educated person that Freire and others in critical pedagogies have sought to inspire. There is the culturally sensitive and respectful educated person that multicultural education has aspired to create (Guilherme, 2002; Sleeter & Grant, 2007). Success in these areas might be difficult to define or measure using the narrow constructs and contexts in which teachers and students are currently evaluated, and it is likely that "success" (as it is construed in an economic context) would not be an appropriate part of the discourse were the emphases in education to shift in these directions. It is challenging to imagine, for example, how success in compassion might be understood, or how it would be appropriate to measure critical cultural awareness. Additionally, it would also be important to problematize ideals such as cultural sensitivity, respect, and care, even as we accept them as representatives of an alternate paradigm of education. Unproblematized, such terms have the potential to become part of hegemonic discourse (in the way that Ellsworth, 1989, and Gore, 1993, cautioned us about the discourse of critical pedagogy), or meaningless and trite, tending toward lip service more than inspired purpose and action. Even more challenging would be to imagine how such capacities in an educated person would be aligned with American culture's geopolitical and economic interests.

In the public conversation, the focus on what students should learn, how they learn it, and what they should know and be able to do with their learning has often had less to do pedagogy than with politics. Competitive, market-based, corporate and nation-state ideas about power and profit have demanded that we continue to label the results of education as successes and failures of our students and educators, irrespective of the roles that forces such as educational funding and social issues have played. It is politically disadvantageous to acknowledge that factors such as poverty, prejudice and protectionism have exacted heavy burdens on the capacity for students and teachers to achieve full voice in education. Despite the calls for equality in education, for leaving no child behind, or for establishing higher standards and educational choice, there is no mention of standards for effecting the social changes that would have far-reaching affects upon the daily life and the futures of our students—standards to which not just schools, but public officials and private citizens would all be held accountable. Accountability in our neoliberal, free-market based economy has de-emphasized the responsibility of the government to provide funding in programs that exist for the benefit of citizens, and instead has shifted attention to the surveillance of what Mark Olssen (1996) referred to as "manipulatable man," citizens who are "perpetually responsive" to the needs of the state, who are subject to "new forms of vigilance, surveillance, [and] 'performance appraisal,' where the state has taken it upon itself to keep us all up to the mark" (p. 340), as we become, in Foucault's terms "*homo oeconomicus* ... entrepreneurs of ourselves," producing our own capital.

Summum ius summa iniuria

As Werner Jaeger (1986a) stated in his landmark study of Greek *paideia*,[6] "education always needs standards" (p. 302). Jaeger traced the movement in ancient standards of education as a simultaneous looking back at foundations in traditional ideals and values about life (mostly gleaned from religion) and a gaze to the future, toward a newer humanistic ideal that emerged in Classical Greece. Education in America has likewise reflected shifts in cultural beliefs about the purpose of education. The standards-based reform movement, which found its beginning after the publication of *A Nation at Risk,* developed in response to the equation of economic competitiveness with educational quality as determined by international comparisons of student performance on (Gardner, 1983; Lee & Ready, 2009). Since the 1980s in America, educational standards have been designed to be guidelines that are useful in the design of curriculum, instruction and assessment for learning, ideally in ways that help educators and students develop vision, purpose, and understanding. In recent decades, discourses about educational standards in the United States have represented strong ideological stances regarding the purposes of education, stances that significantly reflect the contextualized ideas about foundational beliefs in our society, of ideas such as political and religious freedom, democracy and democratic participation. As such, we must recognize any standards as the political device they are, and engage in the challenging, difficult work of recognizing and resisting their hegemonic potential.

In Foucault's (1975) description in *Surveiller et punir* [To discipline and to punish] of society's practices that assert power over people and institutions through disciplinary control and normalization, the examination works most fully to establish power and truth:

> *L'examen combine les techniques de la hiérarchie qui surveille et celles de la sanction qui normalise. Il est un regard normalisateur, une surveillance qui permet de qualifier, de classer et de punir. Il établit sur les individus une visibilité à travers laquelle on les différencie et on les sanctionne. C'est pourquoi, dans tous les dispositifs de discipline, l'examen est hautement ritualise. En lui viennent se rejoindre la cérémonie du pouvoir et la forme de l'expérience, le deployment de la force et l'etablissement de la vérité.* (p. 217)

The examination combines the techniques of hierarchy that monitor and those of punishment that normalize. It is a normalizing gaze, an oversight that allows description, classification and penalty. It establishes upon individuals a visibility through which one differentiates and sanctions them. It is why, in all the devices of discipline, the examination is highly ritualized. In it comes the rejoining of the ceremony of power and the form of experience, the deployment of force and the establishment of truth.

Because of the connection of power to accountability and its standardized tests and measurements, there is ample reason to problematize the relationships among data, measurement, and student achievement on the one hand, and teaching and learning and what is reproduced in schools on the other. In other words, in the environment created by high-stakes testing and data-driven decision making, schools and the processes and people involved in them will tend to reproduce more of what we believe we observe in the data.[7] To better understand the relationship between standardization and the reform agenda in education and reproduction in society, it is useful to consider what Apple (2004), using Raymond William's description of hegemony, reminds us about regarding the need to situate the relationships, practices and mechanisms employed by society within the "complex, stratified, and unequal society" in which they reside (p. 3). Williams wrote that hegemony existed as "a whole body of practices and expectations ... that constitute a sense of reality for most people in the society" (as cited in Apple, 2004, p. 5). Therefore, regarding the hegemony of accountability and measurement in education, it is not merely a matter that a few in power believe that standards, measurement and evaluation are essential to reform; rather, as Apple might describe it, such hegemonic practices and expectations have "saturated" the American collective consciousness (p. 4). Further, as Sizer (1996) observed, there is an "implicit assumption that Americans agree about the purposes of education" (p. 110); therefore, we also accept that national and state standards exist to enact the requirements of this assumption.

The similarities between corporate models of management that rely on data to measure achievement and manage production and federal mandates of education under the No Child Left Behind Act and the recent Race To The Top initiative offer evidence that the "collective consciousness" continues to maintain that education can and should still be evaluated for productivity in the same way that corporations tend to evaluate productivity, a belief that has been in force since mass public schooling was instituted as a means of training a burgeoning population for work in industry. As constructs such as "data" and "standards" have taken center stage in the drama concerning the state of public education, policymakers and politicians continue to seek uniformity, rather than equity, as the solution to the "achievement gap" and for our students' comparatively low rankings on international assessments (which has been used by politicians and the media as evidence of our flawed educational system). Despite a decade of testing and at least two decades of curriculum standards being in place, not to mention a precedent for testing and standardization that spans at least four decades, current rhetoric continues to froth about accountability as if it were a fresh concept; the media, politicians, corporate executives and educators use have used the term to define the first decade of the twenty-first century. A quick web search of the term "Age of Accountability" yields a vast and wide variety of books, journal articles and websites devoted to understanding education in an

"Age of Accountability."[8] In her keynote address at the 2005 China-U.S. conference on Aligning Assessment With Instruction, held in Beijing, Betsy J. Case (2005), director of research and product support for Pearson, Inc. argued that "In the U.S., the 'Age of Accountability' has arrived, heralded by No Child Left Behind. High levels of achievement, as measured by standardized achievement tests, form the cornerstone of the accountability movement in education" (p. 3). Pearson, it must be noted, has been developing products that have driven the accountability movement forward, including data management software, assessments, curriculum (primarily in the form of textbook series), "knowledge technologies;" etc. Most recently, it published a white paper (Jones & Vickery, 2011) with its recommendations for designing the new assessments that will almost inevitably follow the development of the national *Common Core State Standards* (CCSS). "'Along with this new era in student learning brought on by the adoption of the CCSS, comes a new day in testing as states and consortia strive to produce higher quality assessments for assessing student progress toward successfully meeting those standards,' said Walter 'Denny' Way, Ph.D., Senior Vice President, Assessment and Information Group of Pearson'" (Pearson, 2011). Other corporations operating in education, like Pearson, have held privileged seats at the reform table—Achieve, Inc., the Gates Foundation, the Educational Testing Service, and others partnered with the National Governors Association and the Council of Chief State School Officers to create the CCSS. On the other hand, teacher unions, higher education (especially teacher preparation programs), and teachers have not had the same degree of privilege in the reform conversation, and instead have become rather easy targets for blame and have been victimized by the virulent rhetoric of reform.

τῷ δ' ἐνὶ θυμῷ θῆκε μένος καὶ θάρσος

Foucault's (2003, 1961/2006) concepts of the historical-political origins of other institutions such as mental health and prisons offer us frameworks for the contextualized production of standards, which must be understood within in the many dimensions that produce them. Acceptance of standards without a critical stance implies a kind of blindness to the reality of their effects on education and society. The hegemony of standards and standardization promotes inherently discriminatory notions that equate "sameness" with "fairness" (Goulah, 2010). Holding all students accountable for demonstrating the same knowledge in the same manner emphasizes the value of content over context or personal capacity. Valuing standardized testing as a means of measuring success in teaching and learning is a characteristic of current education reform that suggests that it is in some way easier to justify "dreamings about being" than to engage in the complexities of critical examination.

From a critical perspective, national content-area standards can be as dangerous as the reform movement of which they are symptoms. The *Common Core State Standards* have established a de facto hierarchy among concepts and content that could or should be taught, as they unquestioningly privilege math and language arts as priority areas. The standards documents have determined the answers before any critical questions could be posed regarding who gets to decide what is important for students to learn, know, and be able to do with their knowledge. It is not merely a matter of standards determining the rules of the "truth game," to use Foucault's (2000, 2001) term, that is, "the set of procedures that lead to a certain result, which on the basis of its principles and rules of procedure, may be considered valid or invalid, winning or losing" (p. xvi). The dangers become readily apparent when one considers the current movement that attempts to quantify teaching and learning (such as the dubious "value-added" approach to measuring teacher effectiveness), using measures that are so fraught with ambiguity and do not necessarily reveal valid conclusions about teaching and learning, particularly when results are categorized as, in effect, "winning or losing."

There is also the problem of recognizing and confronting the dominance that is inevitably present in the myriad interactions in teaching and learning, interactions that serve to subjugate educators and educated alike, but also present "dangerous" opportunities for critical examination. It is not surprising that, given the weight of the demand for reform and the notions of deficiency applied to teacher and student performances, teacher and student voices in the reform movement have been nearly nonexistent, or have been drowned out by the more strident voices of the well-connected and well-heeled in politics and industry. In the current political and social environment, standards may be envisioned as a fulcrum, balancing the demands of a public requiring reform, and the desire among educators for frameworks within which to design how and what they do in schools and classrooms.

The consideration of the effects of standardization and standards provides a background for the critique of the foreign language, and specifically classical language, learning standards that follows, using Foucauldian and critical pedagogy perspectives as the basis for the critique. It is important to note that Classical language education in its current state maintains a tenuous position in most secondary schools where it is still included in curricula. There is a distinct possibility that Classics may cease to survive in a society that has as its educational focus to produce career- and workforce-ready citizens who can propel its economy out of recession so that it may "win the future" through more training in the so-called STEM (the acronym for science, technology, engineering and math) disciplines (Office of the Press Secretary, 2011). Further, since foreign language education continues to be excluded from what are labeled the core disciplines (math, science, reading and English language arts, and social studies), we may anticipate that the a version of *Common Core State Standards* and associated assessments in this area may not be developed any time soon. This may represent some advantage for foreign language education (and again, Classics specifically), in terms of the autonomy maintained by states, local districts and teachers to design programs, curriculum, instruction and assessment that is not subject to a Foucauldian "normalizing gaze." However, such exclusion also solidifies the continued marginalization of foreign language education and its teachers in the educational life of the United States. Still, the possibilities for the study and promotion of resistance to the effects of power and domination through foreign language education are perhaps unique. As Ortega (1999) points out, there are at least two realities that shape professional identities and practices in language education: societal attitudes toward language, and issues regarding ownership of language and culture (p. 22), and these issues are inextricably linked to the responsibilities of language educators for unmasking the ways in which language works to define and maintain social status, reinforce ideology, and reproduce oppression and oppressive practices (see Blackledge, 2000; Canagarajah, 2005a, 2005b; Guilherme, 2002; Reagan, 2010; Reagan & Osborn, 2002). Therefore, a critical view of both the *National Standards in Foreign Language Education* (2006) and the *Standards for Classical Language Learning* (American Classical League [ACL], 1997) opens pathways to empowerment for both students and educators as they engage together in the work of understanding key critical questions, beginning with: (1) what the contextual basis is for the standards—what are the historical, political or cultural constructs within which they have emerged; (2) whose standards are they—whom do they represent, whom do they serve, and whom do they exclude; (3) what benefits exist in standards, and who can take advantage of those benefits—or, conversely, what do the standards omit or inhibit; and (4) what types of skills, knowledge and capacities do the standards privilege, and which do they marginalize. In a critical pedagogy of foreign language education, learners are encouraged to pose problems that may expose the hidden curriculum beneath the visible curriculum, question the roles and uses of language, examine representations of languages and cultures, analyze the social, political and ideological messages established in language classrooms, textbooks, and other instructional materials, and notions of "fluency," "proficiency," "mastery" and other measures used to describe a range of language skills (Reagan & Osborn, 2002; Wink, 2004).

Unde venis?

A critical analysis of the national foreign and classical language standards can begin with an examination of the standards' influence on educational practices (including, at a minimum, curriculum development and instructional practices) as a Foucauldian discourse that creates the reality within which it operates, in reciprocal relationship with ideology. Michael Apple (2004) has pointed out the importance of situating knowledge, school, and education itself within the social conditions that have caused them to exist. Therefore, part of the work of critical perspective is to reveal, and subsequently unravel, the ideological bonds that restrict what is possible to think, to know, to do and to teach in a given temporal or local context. As many have pointed out (see, e.g., Canagarajah, 2005a, 2005b; Kubota, 2004; Lin, 2004; A. Luke, 2004; Pennycook, 2004b; Osborn, 2000; Pavlenko,2003; Reagan, 2002a; Reagan & Osborn, 2002), the teaching of foreign language has been subject to political and ideological constraints on what languages are most important to teach, who should learn them and for what purposes. Despite the "centrality of language to human life," as Reagan (2009b) points out, the availability of and access to language instruction has often been restricted by concerns related to academic relevance, national defense, and economic competitiveness or dominance. Despite the potential for foreign language study to mitigate cultural isolation, to expand one's perception of reality, or to provide new contexts for "organizing the world" (Reagan, 2009), marginalization of foreign languages and the hegemony of English in the public school curriculum has prevailed (see the study by Rhodes & Pufahl, 2009, on the state of foreign language teaching in the United States), even in, or perhaps especially because of, the reform movement that began with establishment of standards as a method of educational reform.

Foreign language education was the last subject area to receive federal funding for the establishment of standards under the under the Bush/ Clinton era educational initiatives. The task force that developed the standards worked with representatives from education, business, government and other community members to achieve "an unprecedented consensus … on the definition and role of foreign language instruction in American education" (*National Standards in Foreign Language Learning*, 2006). The "consensus" that foreign language educators sought with representatives from business and government leaves little doubt that the "marketized systems" (Apple, 2001) are operating in foreign language education as in other aspects. Given the place of foreign language education, on the margins of the educational terrain, it is worth noting that much of the foreign language standards document reflects elements of the discourses discussed previously, particularly those related to competition. In describing the purposes and uses of foreign language education, the authors of the national standards note that students study languages for myriad reasons, but the first example they give is the pursuit of careers in the international marketplace or government service, and while the desire to learn more about other cultures and other people or to enjoy the cognitive benefits of language learning is included, so too is the need to fulfill a graduation requirement. This description is symptomatic, in part, of reasons why foreign language instruction is so often unsuccessful (Reagan & Osborn, 2002) in developing linguistic or cultural competence: it appears that attention to the context in which language learning occurs may be insufficient, too narrow for meeting the expansive requirements of language learning that would lift American students above the pervasive, hegemonic monolingualism of the United States. Further, planning and policy in language education in the United States has generally not been focused on the empowerment of bilingual or English language learners, nor has it asserted any function for language education that would approach a critical language awareness, in which issues regarding linguistic legitimacy, inequity, or social justice are effectively explored (Reagan & Osborn, 2002). Ortega (1999), citing studies by MacKay and Wong (1988),[11] and Lamb (1994),[12] warns that "without an explicit understanding of context and the politics of teaching languages, teachers are left without the tools to resist hegemonic practices in language education." (p. 23). Beyond personal economic success or satisfaction (recall Foucault's *homo oeconomicus*), there is apparently little justification for foreign language learning in the United States.

Otherization or dominance over "other" is also (perhaps unwittingly) implied in the language used in the *National Standards* to describe the purposes and the "Five C's" of foreign language education. As noted above, students are encouraged to seek greater understanding of "other people and other cultures," to both "master" the language and "[master] the cultural context in which the language occurs (*National Standards for Foreign Language Learning*, 2006, p. 2). One may wonder what it is to "master" language or culture (or whether it would be possible or appropriate to achieve mastery over either), and while it would be inappropriate (and likely inaccurate) to assert that the authors of the standards intentionally or overtly promoted domination over "other" in their description, such word choice points to the almost unavoidable tendency of Americans to approach language and culture within hegemonic contexts. Ruiz (1988) described three angles from which language education has been viewed in the United States, all of which reflect dominant ideologies that have structured all varieties of language education: language-as-problem, where policies are devised when linguistic diversity represents a challenge, either to the dominant culture (of English speakers in the

United States, answered in the form of English-only policies) or to those who must gain access to a society's resources and opportunities; language-as-right, which concerns the extent to which speakers of languages other than English have the right to use their native language; and language-as-resource, where knowledge and competence in languages is recognized as an asset for personal or national economic growth or competitiveness, and less frequently as a means for bilingual or English language learners to act as resources for English speakers attempting to learn languages other than English (see also Ortega, 1999). In the *National Standards for Foreign Language Learning*, there is little that serves as impetus to critically challenge the discourse in any of these areas. Even the attempt made by the *Standards'* authors to address language rights, obliquely referenced in the Statement of Philosophy's declaration that, "Children who come to school from non-English backgrounds should also have opportunities to develop further proficiencies in their first language" fails to attempt to protect such rights, and at best offers only an ambiguous suggestion to educators. The statement itself raises several questions that are of significant import if policymakers or educators endeavor to act on such philosophical grounds. For example, what are the "further proficiencies" in non-English supposed to represent, and by whom should such proficiency be determined or evaluated? What and whose purposes should the development of such proficiencies serve? The phrase "in their first language" is dangerously vague: does it imply that instruction designed to develop some type of language proficiency ought to be conducted in the children's first language, or does it mean that the proficiencies developed would enhance students' knowledge of their first language? The interpretation of this phrase could work to either acknowledge language rights to some degree (if instruction were conducted in children's first language), or could impose more restrictions on children's experience of their first language (by attempting to educate to develop a child's first language in some way that might assert English-language linguistic dominance). Implicit in this statement is an acknowledgement that while children "should" be given such opportunities, policies and politics will likely not commit to granting them.

While the establishment of national standards may have allowed foreign language education entry into the wider educational reform movement in the 1990s, and while the standards themselves have served to articulate many important aspects of language education and to provide guidance to educators wishing to unify under such a guiding light, they must still be subject to critical scrutiny. There is clearly some room within the standards within which to develop a vision for a social justice agenda in foreign language education. However, the standards are missing much more direct, explicit connection to those elements that Freire and others would include to advance conscientization. For example, the standards promote an "anthropological" understanding of culture, achieved by understanding the relationships between practices, products and perspectives of the target language's culture. However, how culture is defined or understood is much more complex than an outsider's (or anthropological) view might account for. As students of foreign language set about determining for themselves the relationships among practices, products and perspectives, they must also recognize the impact they have as observers, and their own position in those relationships. The "culture" of the Five C's may inspire critical questioning of the assumptions teachers and learners bring to encounters with practices, products and perspectives, but there is no explicit invitation to explore such questions, and that leaves open the possibility of a deepening otherization of culture. Further, it must be acknowledged that the *Standards* exist to unify foreign language teaching and learning, not bilingual, ESL and foreign language education. Instead, the foreign language standards enhance the double-standard that exists in the consciousness and practices of language education, in which bilingual and ESL education exist to compel students to acquire academic, "native-like" competency in standard English language, while English-language students come to foreign language learning later in their lives as "an elite endeavor," by choice, with little of the push to achieve proficiency that ESL students encounter (Ortega, 1999; Reagan & Osborn, 2002).

Et tu?

The ACL and the APA joined forces after the creation of the *National Standards for Foreign Language Learning* (2006) to create what they referred to as a companion document to the national standards that would address more specifically teaching and learning of ancient Greek and Latin. While the classical task force embraced the national standards as "visionary," "world class," and "realistic but attainable," they determined that classical language education required an interpretation of the goals and standards that would be specific to ancient languages. At the same time, they sought to "position classicists to play a role in standards-based reform" (ACL, 1997 p. 2), an acknowledgement of the fact that, even within the area of foreign language education, classical language education remains on the margin. Since the precipitous decline of classical language instruction that occurred steadily throughout the nineteenth and most of the twentieth century, the reawakening of interest and enrollments in Latin in the 1990s prompted the task force to declare in the classical standards document that classical language learning maintains its appeal "not [because of] political or economic interests … but [because of] educational beliefs that do not go out of style" (p. 3). Whether Classics is outside or within the bounds of "style" in education or not, in defending its contemporary appeal, this statement also acknowledges Classics' challenges in the face of changing educational contexts. As Classics and classicists continue to seek distance from the discipline's association with an élitist past and economic or political power, the introduction to the classical standards declares that "Latin is for all students," citing the programs begun in inner city and impoverished students to "boost academic success" through Latin learning (p. 3).

In the case of the classical standards, the "other" is the ancient world; we teachers and learners position ourselves in relation to the offerings of language and culture of the ancients that serve to illuminate our understanding of a Western heritage, as we are supposed to receive information from Greeks and Romans who, in "breaking barriers of time and place, have communicated their messages through the ages" (p. 4). In some respects, this concept of "other" may be less inclined toward hegemony than the "other" that the modern standards establish. As classical languages are technically "dead," no native speakers exist to provide resistance to our tendency to exert or assume our linguistically- or culturally-dominant agenda, or to challenge us to confront our *"foreignness* agenda" described by Osborn (2000, italics in original).[9] Yet, because of the extent to which classical Greek and Latin "live" on in English and Romance languages, and because of the reception model of literary interpretation that has become a major component of scholarly study in Classics, we and our students are provided with myriad opportunities to reflect critically on the agendas, attitudes, and assumptions we bring to language and cultural studies through the reference point of ancient presences. Julia Haig Gaisser (2002), in her outstanding work on the reception of the ancient Roman poet Catullus in the Renaissance, describes the opportunities classical texts present to readers of every era in this way:

> Classical texts are not only moving but changing targets…. [They] are not teflon-coated baseballs hurtling through time and gazed up at uncomprehendingly by the natives of various times and places, until they reach our enlightened grasp; rather, they are pliable and sticky artifacts gripped, molded, and stamped with new meanings by every generation of readers and they come to us irreversibly altered by their experience. (p. 387)

For classical language students and their teachers, there is not merely language and/or literature study—there is also the situated, contextual examination of the frameworks we bring to bear on classical works, rife with questions that have great potential to illuminate our cultural and temporal contexts and biases. As Reagan (2002a) reminds us,

The Greeks sought answers to the most fundamental questions of human existence—questions about the good life, justice, knowledge, ethics, and so on. These are the questions at the heart of the "human conversation," and it is here that the goals of critical pedagogy and those of classics, and indeed, of education in general, coalesce. (pp. 32-33)

Osborn's (2000) claim that the "exigencies of providing quality language education in the United States necessitate addressing critical reflection in world language education" appears to exclude Latin language education from the avenues through which the *"foreignness* agenda may be transformed (p. 113). However, it is still possible to "macrocontextualize," or to connect, curriculum and instruction to the societal milieu in which language education occurs in classical language learning, and options for such contextualization in classical languages will be explored in the next chapter. Perhaps more importantly for this discussion, Reagan's (2009a) contention that language study is important for understanding how we perceive and apprehend reality through linguistic structures and constraints is most instructive for the sake of considering the context in which classical language learning may be transformative.

Cui bono?

Osborn (2006) and others (see, e.g., Oxford, 2010) view the *Standards* as a platform from which to grow reform in foreign language teaching, though Osborn acknowledges that national standards may also serve as a means of reproducing forms of cultural domination. Through "aggressively pursuing the ideals embodied in the standards" (p. 9), rejecting hierarchical approaches to curriculum development, and incorporating the historic, regional, ethical and contexts in which education occurs Osborn contends, it is possible to create a critical pedagogy of foreign language education. The Five C's of foreign language education—communication, cultures, connections, comparisons, and communities—offer a reasonable backdrop for goals for foreign language learning, and the alliteration perhaps provides a convenient means of encapsulating these goals.

However, the Five C's, the standards they express, and the way they are articulated in the *Standards* document are not neutral, and they provide opportunities to pursue other critical questions. For example, the authors of the *National Standards* asserted the following: "Knowing how, when, and why to say what to whom" represents "all the linguistic and social knowledge required for effective human-to-human interaction" (*National Standards for Foreign Language Learning*, 2006, p. 3). This statement begs the question, "For whose purpose(s), or from whose perspective, is this the case?" This is a fundamental question to pursue in a critical pedagogy of foreign language—the generalized "all" provokes a critical examination of who benefits from the policies the standards inevitably generate en route to creating curricular paths.[10] For example, who benefits from knowing "how, when and why to say."—the speaker or the recipient of the speech? Further, what social purposes do these points of knowledge serve, and what power structures do they preserve or enforce? The "when" and "why" questions refer the context in which the speech occurs, but do not account for the "who" present on both sides of the interaction, and there is an implicit assumption that those who lack such knowledge suffer some consequence of ineffective interaction, and that the consequences are reasonable. Further, one may question why speech is privileged in this statement, and to what extent the foreign language standards place an emphasis on speaking as the dominant language skill in human interaction. For those for whom speech or aural/oral communication is a challenge or is impossible, we must understand that they may find themselves marginalized in the world of language learning.

The privileging of oral communication as a method in language teaching, and as an outcome for language learners, has been seen in recent discussions in classical language (in the case of this study, Latin particularly, and to some extent ancient Greek) pedagogy. Second language acquisition methodologies emphasized in recent decades in modern language pedagogy, such as Krashen and Terrell's (1983) "natural approach," have focused on enhancing aural comprehension and oral communication as a means of allowing students to internalize and access the functions and structures of second languages in ways similar to first language acquisition. In some of the most vigorous electronic discussions (on Internet listserves such as *Latinteach*, online groups such as latin-bestpractices@yahoo.com, and blogs that serve as fora for Latin learning, such as Latinum), advocates of the so-called "active" use of Latin in classrooms (primarily via oral communication methods) have increasingly called for oral components on standardized tests such as the advanced placement examination in Latin, and oral proficiency examinations for new Latin teachers, components that would to some extent resemble the requirements that modern language learners and teachers are accountable for on such assessments. While there may be much value for some students of classical languages to engage in the learning of Latin and Greek in part through aural/oral methods, the push to standardize or to routinize such practices in classical language education sets the stage for, at a minimum, potentially irrelevant or artificial imposition of modern language pedagogy, in the hopes that students are reminded that Latin is a language, rather than a code waiting to be deconstructed. While "conversational Latin" yields some potentially engaging educational moments, and there is the possibility that communicating in Latin vivifies the perceived deadness of Latin, communicating in the manner of modern culture's tableaus (such as constructing conversations about finding a good automobile mechanic) might yield less for the learner than direct engagement with the Latin or Greek they hope to ultimately be able to read. Most classical language learners have relatively limited time in which to learn enough language to acquire enough proficiency in reading to access the work of ancient authors. Some have argued, however, that traditional instructional methods used in classical language education have not allowed all students to be successful in acquiring skills and knowledge required to read Latin. Speech may activate for many students an effective means of comprehending and using linguistic patterns seen in the Latin or Greek texts classical language learners hope to be able to read, and many teachers of classical languages have used spoken or "active" Latin successfully in this way (see, e.g., Neuman, 2008). Further, incorporation of oral Latin or Greek in the classroom has represented in the classical language community an opportunity to move away from traditional approaches viewed as stale, dogmatic, or ineffective (in particular, "grammar-translation" method of instruction has been labeled as such) and toward newer, perhaps more innovative practices. Still, standardizing the incorporation of an oral communication component, in the teaching or learning of classical languages, in an attempt to solidify its place in classical pedagogy, ignores the needs of at least some students for whom auditory or phonological processing is challenging (who may seek opportunities to learn foreign languages through methods that do not require heavy amounts of aural/oral communication).[13] It also asserts the imposition of psycholinguistic models of language acquisition that have been applied in "living" languages that may not necessarily be appropriate for "dead" languages. It may be argued that the application of such models as the "natural approach" in classical language pedagogy moves Classics perhaps further down the path of its marginalization in foreign language education. Since there are no native speakers of Latin and Greek, one cannot seek them out to provide for classical language learners the same sort of authentic experience of communication in language that may occur in modern languages in encounters with native speakers.

Of course, similar arguments may be levied against the privileging of any one method or skill over another in language learning, especially if we do not raise critical questions about its implications or potential to perpetuate obstacles to learning or access to knowledge. Perhaps more to the point, advocacy of one pedagogical method or another, or a particular skill, and an insistence on standardization and measurement of such, appears to be more representative of the objectification of language that advocates technicist approaches to addressing challenges in classical language education that do not really have their bases in technical issues (see Reagan, 2002a, 2009a). Oral, active, spoken Latin or ancient Greek may inspire lively lessons and engaged learning for some students and others who study these languages. However, we must avoid the impulse to define or make claims and judgments about the purposes of using spoken language and skill levels of such in ways that seek to objectify the language. As Reagan has argued (2009a),

> When we engage in teaching languages, our goal is to move the student's linguistic behavior in the foreign language closer to the preconceived norms of the singular reality of that target language. What we do, in short, is to engage in the objectification, or reification, of the construct of "language," which in turn has led us to misunderstand the nature of language and to accept what are essentially technicist views of the teaching and learning of languages. (p. 4)

Given the context of the drive to establish standards that unify language education practices, codify language knowledge and skills, which arguably are problematic as much as they serve as a resource for curriculum development (and inevitably impact the design of assessments for measuring such knowledge and skills), it is not only appropriate but necessary to question the impact of the imposition of oral language skill requirements for dead languages.

In any case, the experience of learning classical languages is full of uniquely valuable, authentic encounters with language and culture that transcend measurement or quantification. In fact, as Farrell (2001) describes the experience of learning Latin, "it is the culture *embodied by* the language to which all who study and value Latinity belong" (p. 7, italics in original). In effect, we moderns become natives in Latinity, as:

> The business of learning Latin, reading Latin, studying and writing about Latin, even remembering … one's school Latin or thinking of the language only occasionally, is bound up in shared experiences, patterns of oppositions, persistent prejudices. To encounter Latin nowadays is to belong to this culture, which is larger and more heterogeneous than one might expect it to be. (p. 7)

In this respect, classical language learners may enjoy an "insider's view" on a culture of classical language learning, an intersection in language and culture that modern foreign language learners may never be privy to. If we accept Farrell's notion that those who study Latin inevitably shape a culture of Latinity, unique to their day, then we may also accept that Latinists should "abandon any pretense to a disinterested perspective on a past culture that is wholly Other" (p. 8). Unlike an anthropological view of culture, which both the *National Standards for Foreign Language Learning* (2006) and the *Standards for Classical Language Learning* (ACL, 1997) appear to focus on, with language learners as outsiders learning about foreign cultures' perspectives through products and practices, the classical language learner's access to culture is through a "past rooted in the here and now" (Farrell, 2002, p. 8). The "C" of communication in the classical language standards establishes reading as the "first standard and the key to communicating with the ancient world" with oral, listening skills, and writing practice used to support the goal of reading ancient texts (ACL, 1997, p. 7). The "C" of culture is accessed through encounters with classical literature and physical artifacts. However, such encounters with communication and culture become problematic in the case of Latin; we ought not to believe that the Latin we read in ancient texts is the same language spoken by the Romans. As Farrell (2002) points out, and as Adams' study (2003) of bilingualism and the Latin language reveals, the Latin of written record is "a strange and unusual thing, a language so artificial that it cannot serve the purposes of transient, everyday speech; it is an artificial language, and not a natural one" (p. 18). In Vergil, the Roman "race" is founded by the Trojan Aeneas, in fulfillment of a destiny dictated by the gods, a race that Jupiter prophesied would rule the world widely and for a long time. But Aeneas was a foreigner, a fugitive by fate (*fato profugus*), not a native. No myth establishes an autochthonous Roman people; as Farrell says, "All members of Latin culture must journey to Rome, each in his or her own way; we modern Latins are in this respect no different from any other member of our culture at any time, in any place" (p. 27). In particular, "modern Latins" in American culture may find resonance in the story of cultural journeying and transplanting: just as there may be no native Romans, dominant culture in America is likewise not of native origin. Thus, when we seek to understand the perspectives of Roman culture in the practices and products of the Romans, we are compelled to consider the historical contexts of those perspectives and how, why and by whom they were constructed, in order to avoid a facile, totalizing conception of who the Romans were. Farrell's assertion that there is a modern culture of Latinity, established and reestablished, written and re-written throughout the centuries by each generation that encounters the linguistic structures, expression and ideas of Latin's written form aligns with Foucault's concept of "archeology," which establishes discourse as the factor that controls what is possible to say, think, know in the context of an historical present. Problematization of the amorphous concept of culture may yield much fruitful exploration for students and teachers of classical languages if we choose to avoid linear paths among perspectives, products and practices, and instead see these facets of culture within a framework that uncovers historical relations of discourse, power and knowledge.

We may apply a similar, Foucauldian lens to a view of the remaining C's (Connections, Comparisons, and Communities) of the *Standards for Classical Language Learning* (ACL, 1997). Comparisons and connections are perhaps almost inevitable in encounters with language and culture— many differences and correspondences are readily apparent. In some respects, examination of comparisons and connections elucidates certain types of information about ourselves and our place in the world, much of which may be valuable for self-knowledge, for understanding of dimensions of human existence, and, in a practical sense, for the justification of language study in curriculum. Students and teachers of classical languages often reflect on the interdisciplinary nature of classical studies, which can serve to illuminate concepts, events and systems in the modern world (ACL, 1997, p. 13). There is great merit in understanding the indebtedness of Western and American heritage to classical models as a means of acquiring perspectives, including critical perspectives, on such origins. The classical standards for Comparisons also focus on comparisons of classical language structures and vocabulary to English as a means of acquiring a better understanding English structures and vocabulary. Certainly, such structural analysis is one way of deepening knowledge of linguistic conventions. However, there are also dangers inherent in focusing on comparisons and connections without a critical viewpoint that questions the nature of the comparisons made, the knowledges that are privileged in connections, and the potential imbalances in power and "truths" that are established. For example, while the standards document states that "by examining and analyzing the public and private lives of the ancient Greeks and Romans, students acquire a perspective from which to examine and analyze their own culture more objectively, one must question if and how this objectivity occurs. Comparison establishes a de facto duality, through emphasizing differences and even through recognizing similarities. Duality leads to the construction of identities based on notions of Self and Other, native and foreign, common and unusual, right and wrong, good and bad. Such dualities are often the foundations for hegemonic practices. From a Foucauldian perspective, curriculum developed around the standard of comparison establishes "a discourse that constitutes and constructs, incites and induces, rather than simply documents and describes, reality" (Parkes, Gore, & Elsworth, 2010, p. 166).

The "C" of Connections is in some ways less problematic than "Comparisons," in that it is the interdisciplinary nature of Classics that may work to counteract or resist potentially hegemonic practices that were once associated with classical education. However, the impulse to locate Classics in a central hub of learning or as a prerequisite for one becoming one of "the learned," as some conservative discourse has tended toward, must be resisted. Such resistance can open avenues for interconnectedness, not only among disciplines, where boundaries of knowledge may be traversed, blurred, and perhaps even eliminated or disempowered, but also in human interactions and encounters. In the examination of connections in classical language curriculum, we may find something beyond the discourse of tolerance as a means of improving human relations and reducing oppression.

Active pursuit of connections may lead not only to intercultural competence that is often a focus of critical language pedagogy, but it may redefine notions and discourse of the final "C": Communities. The curricular concept of "communities" in the classical language standards is either intentionally or necessarily vague, and reflects more the elements of the other C's in promoting awareness of Latin and Greek in local and "global" communities through communication and connection. The potential strength of the "Communities" standard is that it can be interpreted in the classical standards as the expression of a responsibility for participation, even activism, on the part of those who study Classics. Though the foundation may be weak (focusing on students "sharing their knowledge of cultural differences in the Greco-Roman world," and "recognizing that cultural diversity has been an integral feature of society since antiquity"), and does not necessarily compel curriculum development or instructional practices that subvert the forces of prejudice, the "Communities" standard does imply that there is a path toward education for social justice that teachers and students of classical languages may follow. Possible avenues for teaching social justice through Classics is the subject of the final chapter of this study.

NOTES

1. The full quote, from *Republic*, 7.533c provides an appropriate backdrop for the some points that will be considered herein:

    αἱ δὲ λοιπαί, ἃς τοῦ ὄντος τι ἔφαμεν ἐπιλαμβάνεσθαι, γεωμετρίας τε καὶ τὰς ταύτῃ ἑπομένας, ὁρῶμεν ὡς ὀνειρώττουσι μὲν περὶ τὸ ὄν, ὕπαρ δὲ ἀδύνατον αὐταῖς ἰδεῖν, ἕως ἂν ὑποθέσεσι χρώμεναι ταύτας ἀκινήτους ἐῶσι, μὴ δυνάμεναι λόγον διδόναι αὐτῶν. ᾧ γὰρ ἀρχὴ μὲν ὃ μὴ οἶδε, τελευτὴ δὲ καὶ τὰ μεταξὺ ἐξ οὗ μὴ οἶδεν συμπέπλεκται, τίς μηχανὴ τὴν τοιαύτην ὁμολογίαν ποτὲ ἐπιστήμην γενέσθαι;

    Those sciences [mathematics], which we have said have an apprehension of being- geometry and the like—are, we see, only dreamings about being. But for them to reveal the full waking reality is impossible, as long as they leave untouched the hypotheses they use, and do not themselves have the ability to tell the full story. For when one does not know the starting point, and when the conclusion and what is between are constructed from points not known, by what device can such consensus become scientific knowledge?

So, mathematics (and measurement in general, to clarify my argument) may be superior to conjecture or opinion in revealing some aspects of reality, but such science falls short of dialectic in an absence of critical questioning.

2. This recalls the quote attributed to Einstein that "not everything that can be counted counts, and not everything that counts can be counted." Business and management strategists adapted and widely embraced a version of this too: "What gets measured gets done" (attributed variously to Peter Drucker, Tom Peters, etc.). As education's attempts to design schooling according to corporate models has continued through the twenty-first century, we have seen elements of Drucker's "management by objectives" concepts (Drucker, 1993) influence educational practices from the classroom to the board room, in the use of data for managing processes ("if you can't measure it, you can't manage it"), for establishing goals and identifying progress. The so-called "S.M.A.R.T. goals, often used in education for everything from strategic school planning to lesson planning, are often attributed to elements of Drucker's Management by Objectives, or MBO, organizational management theory). It is interesting to note that a classic controversy in business management theory involved interpretations of Drucker's MBO, with its focus on goal setting and organizational productivity, and William Edwards Deming's Total Quality Management, or TQM (see Carson, 1993), and its focus on quality as the means of improving organizations. Deming (2000) insisted that "management by numerical goal" (as in MBO) was "an attempt to manage without knowledge of what to do, and in fact is usually management by fear." He contended, "It is easier for a ... manager to short-circuit his need for learning and his responsibilities, and instead to focus on the far end, to focus on the outcome.... Focus on outcome is not an effective way to improve a process or an activity" (p. 76).

3. Calls for reform are nearly as old as public education itself, in the United States. As Glass (2008) points out, "Criticism and reform of the education of young people as old when Quintilian (A.D. 35-95) was young" (p. 4).

4. Berliner and Biddle (1995) famously refuted the notion of crisis in American education, and Glass (2008) asks us to consider what our national focus might be (or might have been during the past 30 years) had it not been on attention to narrow visions of "reform" in response to a crisis that may well not exist, or exist in ways other than the considerations that flood our current consciousness.

5. The Gates Foundation has dedicated millions to fund research into establishing more objective techniques to measure teacher effectiveness. In a recent *New York Times* article, researchers involved in the project indicated that they are attempting to "separate the attributes of good teaching from the idiosyncrasies of individual teaching" (Dillon, 2010, p. A1), by combin-

ing value-added methodology with assessment of teacher content knowledge, student surveys, and digital video recordings of teachers' lessons.

6. Jaeger (1986) describes the Greek word *paideia* as "the shaping of the Greek character" (p. ix). Admitting that such a definition does not truly capture the meaning of paideia, he further explains the concept as a unity of terminology of the modern era such as civilization, culture, tradition, literature and education—all of which refer to, but do not fully represent, aspects of the making of the Greek "cultured man." Jaeger's work represents his attempt to explore the "interaction between the historical process by which [the Greek] character was formed and the intellectual process by which [the Greeks] constructed their ideal of human personality" (p. ix).

7. [7] This recalls "Campbell's Law" (Campbell, 1979), increasingly cited in books (see Nichols & Berliner, 2007), essays and articles (e.g., Rothstein, 2011), and blogs (e.g., Meier, 2007) on the distortions created by high-stakes testing: "The more any quantitative social indicator is used for social decision-making, the more subject it will be to corruption pressures and the more apt it will be to distort and corrupt the social processes it is intended to monitor."

8. Such a search revealed titles that touch on every aspect of education: "Educational Leadership in an Age of Accountability;" "Educational Research in an Age of Accountability;" "The Superintendent in an Age of Accountability;" "Understanding Teacher Stress in an Age of Accountability'" "Building School Culture in an Age of Accountability;" and "Principal Flight in the Age of Accountability."

9. The *"foreignness* agenda is defined by Osborn (2000) "as an expression of sociocultural distinctness growing out of a framework we have discussed as whiteness" (p. 113).

10. Michael Apple (2004) reminds us that knowledge and curriculum are not neutral, and that we must ask the following questions if we are to critically and actively engage with an otherwise "depoliticized" culture distributed by schools: "whose culture," "What social group's knowledge?" and "In whose interest is certain knowledge … taught in cultural institutions like schools?" (p. 15).

11. MacKay and Wong (1988) surveyed journal articles topics in three major professional journals of language education, including *TESOL Quarterly, Modern Language Journal*, and *Foreign Language Annals*, for the purpose of examining frequency of articles published concerning sociopolitical issues in language education.

12. Lamb's (1994) study involved a nation-wide survey of high school, college and university language teachers, which demonstrated the pervasive notion among foreign language educators that language education, including foreign language, bilingual education and ESL was a largely apolitical or impartial endeavor.

13. See Barbara Hill's (n.d.) brochure, "Latin for Students With Learning Disabilities," which briefly summarizes and cites the research that demonstrates that Latin may be an appropriate choice for students with a variety of challenges, including auditory and phonological processing disorders.

CHAPTER 5

HUMANITAS

Classical Studies on the Path of Social Justice

Sed quoniam, ut praeclare scriptum est a Platone, non nobis solum nati sumus ortusque nostri partem patria vindicate, partem amici, atque, ut placet Stoicis, quae in terres gignantur, ad usum hominum omnia creari, hominess autem hominum causa esse generates, ut ipsi inter se aliis alii prodesse possent, in hoc naturam debemus ducem sequi, communes utilitates in medim afferre mutatione officiorum, danda accipiendo, tum artibus, tum opera, tum facultatibus devincire hominum inter homines societatem.

—Cicero (*De Officiis*, 1.22)

Since, as was written famously by Plato, we are not born for ourselves alone, but our country demands part of our birth, and our friends a part; and, as was acceptable to the Stoics, all things that are produced on the earth are created for the use of people, people therefore are also born for the sake of people, so that they are able to benefit each other. In this we ought to follow the lead of nature, to care for the public good, in exchanging responsibilities, in giving and receiving, in skills, in works and in the capacity to unite human society, to join people to one another.

Consiliō et Animīs: Tracing a Path to Social Justice Through the Classics, pp. 97–115
Copyright © 2012 by Information Age Publishing

Cicero composed his last essay, *De Officiis* (On Duties), as the Roman Republic was collapsing around him, to be replaced in short order (and after his assassination) by the form of government the Romans for centuries had abhorred: autocratic empire. Addressed to his son, but very likely meant for a wide audience, *De Officiis* was a lengthy discussion of the application of philosophy and ethics for Roman society, and the obligations of civic and personal responsibility in the preservation of a moral, just state at a time when it was evident, as Cicero admitted, that such concepts were no longer relevant in a society that preferred the expedient to the morally right. While Cicero's own political decisions and positions on what was fair, equitable or just indicate that he would be at best an inconsistent model in any discussion of social justice in modern times, an examination of his writings on such issues offers an accessible place for contemporary Americans to begin to reflect on society's notions of "public good," and our capacity to "unite human society, to join people to one another." Cicero asserts the importance of education in philosophy and rhetoric as a means of acquiring understanding or wisdom about one's moral place in the world; likewise, a critical pedagogy may also yield similar opportunities to engage students and teachers on the path of social justice toward an activism that comes from questioning, dialectic, and reflection.

As students of classical studies, we have an opportunity to view the struggles of ancient individuals and societies from the vantage point that time and distance afford. While "we" are certainly not "them" or even "like them," and though the ancients do not offer us models (in the way that some of the founders regarded the Greeks and Romans), we are still invited to look at, read, contemplate, and wonder about what has been left by them, and what has not, what and who of their culture and society is known or knowable or not, and how generations between their existence and our own have interpreted their lives, mores, and artifacts. As we do so, we can also turn the mirror upon ourselves with the critical perspective we acquire from looking at ourselves gazing at the past. What we notice may inform how we negotiate our modern interactions and illuminate epistemological constructs and contexts. The emergence of research and scholarship in Classics in areas such as feminist perspectives and pedagogy, reception studies, and critical issues in translation, as well as studies of ancient conceptualizations of sexuality, diversity, class, and sociological perspectives on the ancient world demonstrates the great range of critical examinations in which students and scholars of Classics may engage, and which may open doors to the activism in the cycle of praxis in critical pedagogy that is the pursuit of social justice.

As was noted previously, critical pedagogy has been traditionally associated with educational practices that focus on resistance to the forces of domination and oppression in education and in the world. Its praxis engages students and teachers in the critical examination of the effects of politics, economics, ideologies, and social relationships on teaching, learning, curriculum development, professional development, and the physical structures of education. The cycle of praxis (of theory into action) blurs distinctions between the roles of teacher and student, as the work of critical reflection, dialectic and conscientization (critical social conscious-ness) is engaged.

Students and teachers of classical languages and culture may begin their critical reflections with the role of classical education in American society. The legacy of Classics as a tool for teaching the cultural and polit-ical elite and ensuring its continued dominance in the United States can-not be dismissed in a defense of classical education, and its affect as a hegemonic practice does reflect some aspects of Classics' contemporary image problem. Popular perception of classical learning appears to be skewed by its association as a tool of the intellectual elite, the privileged and the conservative, and it is often claimed that the "deadness" of ancient Greek and Latin is a mismatch for the needs of a twenty-first cen-tury education. Yet, classical studies have provided fodder for deep exam-inations of perspectives, ideologies, beliefs, philosophies, cultural dynamics, and so on. that have characterized Western civilization throughout the centuries and which continue to be relevant for modern educators.

For example, the classical civilizations were engaged in many of the hegemonic practices and injustices that characterize aspects of our society today. The Greeks' and Romans' cultural identities were constructed and challenged by interactions with the "Other," as their empires spread throughout the Mediterranean world (Gruen, 2011). Dominance over other cultures and societies did not simply or always imply subjugation, and the relationships among conquerors and the conquered were com-plex in a variety of ways;[1] for the student of Classics, the influence of such encounters on language and culture would be a primary focus. Romans, who were not necessarily concerned with social justice or human rights (at least as modern society may understand these terms) as a practical matter, did consider, at least philosophically, the importance of just treatment of others for the sake of the public good (Bauman, 1999).[2] Although often held up as a model for participatory governance and civic responsibility, Athenians practiced a democracy that excluded the majority of the popu-lation, and which posed for citizens (those who could participate in civic life) certain conflicts in the balance between personal liberty and public obligation (Christ, 2006; Herman, 2006; Liddel, 2007).[3] The political structure of the Roman Republic allowed for representation among all classes of citizens, but was weighted to give heavy advantage to the wealthy patrician class in voting rights. Ancient Greek and Roman societies marginalized the majority of their populations—slaves, women, foreign-born residents, the poor, and so on—and faced serious consequences as a result. Slave revolts, power struggles, internal and external warring, and a burgeoning population of the impoverished posed significant threats to the stability of the Roman state throughout its history. Study of such issues in ancient societies invite comparisons to modern society that are almost irresistible, although we must always be aware of the discourses that constrain the way we think about these issues and comparisons and what is regarded as important about them.[4]

In classical studies, we find many opportunities for critical reflection to inspire social justice. For example, we may begin with the ancient Roman notion of *humanitas*, and construct a modern model of teaching classics for social justice. *Humanitas*, used by Cicero and others to refer to a type of education (in Roman appropriation and adaptation of the Greeks' *paideia*; see Jaeger, 1986; Whitmarsh, 2010) for the commitment to a life of active public service, as a mark of a "cultured" human, was interpreted by later generations as the development of one's humanity, in becoming a "just" human being.[5] A modern concept of *humanitas* implores us to engage with our students in the investigation of institutions, actions and consequences of power, and especially the institutionalized powerlessness among so many on the margins, and to create avenues for liberation.

A model of teaching Classics for social justice must begin with a commitment to transforming what Padraig Hogan (1998) has termed the "partiality of our understanding."[6] Following Socrates' lead in recognizing that in fact we know nothing, and what we believe we know is already tarnished by inadequacies, misconceptions, or prejudices,[7] teachers and student of Classics acquire space for critical self-reflection. Through encounters with myths, histories, narratives, dramas, and letters, we engage in a circumspect examination of ancient and modern conceptions of self and other, of the productive and reproductive effects of power, and of other aspects that are a focus of a critical pedagogy. Using classical studies as a tool for transformation, we have many opportunities to examine the effects of prejudice, ethnocentrism, sexism, racism, conceptions of sexuality, and other issues in society.

Classics remains remarkably relevant for engaging modern students in dialogue about social justice issues. Leaving aside for the moment the wide variety of ancient materials that are available for such critical examinations, we see that today's introductory Latin textbooks are filled with opportunities to explore various "isms" and biases of modern and ancient society. A starting point for engaging in critical questioning with first-time Latin students might be the following: why would textbook editors have created a fictional Roman *familia* for the subject of its series, represented by a wealthy father of the senatorial class, a mother, son, and daughter, when only approximately ten percent of the Roman population would have resembled this configuration? Further, what is the impact of this characterization on students who begin their study of Latin from this perspective? To what extent are such representations alienating to students and their teachers? Students need not even open the textbook to begin to consider who has been marginalized and why.

Of course, ancient texts and other materials offer much more. Consider, for example, Pliny the Younger's letter to Emperor Trajan about his "Christian problem," in which Pliny describes his quandary: as governor of his province, he needs to know what his position should be regarding this radical religious sect that has followers who refuse to pay proper respects to the state gods, and are hence putting the rest of the Roman population in danger of the angry retribution of the gods. Trajan writes back, telling him that those Christians who agree to renounce their faith and participate in religious rites to the Roman gods are to be spared, while those who do not must be fiercely pursued and executed, as they represent a danger to the state (Pliny, *Epistulae* 10.96-97). While we must conscientiously avoid facile comparisons of our modern condition to the ancients', this exchange would likely resonate strongly in the minds of students and teachers who may make connections to the current tensions and rhetoric in the U.S. and Europe surrounding Muslims and Islamic faith.

One cannot read the *Iliad* and *Odyssey* without encountering ideas about human sexuality and notions of shame that may be unfamiliar or even offensive to some, especially those who have beliefs grounded in the notion of homo- or heterosexuality; the Greeks, for their part, did not engage in distinctions of this nature. Greek ideas about the body, the purpose and nature of sex, and the religious connection to both stand in stark contrast to modern ideas and values about them. While it is not within the scope of this study to detail the differences among modern and ancient ideals, let it suffice to say that students and teachers will find fertile ground for the seeds of relevant reflection and critical questioning about the ideas we have assumed about sexuality. As duBois (2001) points out, "Reading the ancient Greeks provides a perspective on our own practices, and on our heritage, putting it into history. Our ideas about sexuality are not natural or inevitable. They are the legacy of a particular development, always in the process of change" (pp. 75-76).

While many cultural and historical issues of classical Greece and Rome are highly relevant to discussions we could or should be having in modern classrooms, there are also issues germane to classical language studies that have a primary role in a critical pedagogy classroom. Indeed, as Reagan (2009a) asserts,

> Language is not merely an intrinsic component of the educational process as the medium of instruction in the classroom, but also services as the mediator of social reality for students and teachers alike. It plays a central role in articulating and conveying not only social, cultural and empirical ideas, but ideological concepts as well. It is also used to make judgments about the speaker, not to mention its role in maintaining differential power relations. (p. vii)

Therefore, the importance of language study is central to establishing a critical pedagogy of Classics. In his book, *Latin Language and Culture*, Joseph Farrell (2001) suggests that the experience of "coming to Latin" in the modern world through developing the ability to read Latin is to gain entry into a culture of "Latinity ... a vast and largely unexplored region of linguistic and social pluralism extending from remotest antiquity down to the present day" (p. xii). From our first encounters with Latin language, we begin to understand the hegemony of formal, written, classical period Latin associated with wealth and power, versus the marginalized, generally spoken, vernaculars of the vulgar crowd. Farrell goes further to assert that we ought to regard classical studies "not as the contemplation of a completely external, independent, objective reality, but as a hermeneutic engagement with a developing entity in which we ourselves are inextricably involved" (p. xiii).

We may look to classical language and culture from the luxury that temporal and spatial distance affords, to safely explore critical questions in an admittedly unsafe world. How much or how little those questions have changed over time is not the most significant thing that classical learning offers. Rather, what we bring to the questions is what matters most. Beard and Henderson (2000) capture the essence of modern interactions with the Classics in this way:

> Of course, Classics is about more than the physical remains, the architecture, sculpture, poetry and paintings, of ancient Greece and Rome. It is also (to select a few things) about the poetry, drama, philosophy, science, and history written in the ancient world, and still read and debated as part of our own culture.... This complex, interactive process of reading, understanding, and debate is itself the challenge of Classics. (pp. 7-8)

Through Classics we can debate our relationship with our own world, with a razor-sharp focus on critical questions, on questioning assumptions about the way things are, on whose shoulders the burden of change and chaos inevitably fall, those constants in a world in which humanity seeks the illusion of control through understanding. For American students, Classics offers a foundation for a dialogue and engagement in a praxis that illuminates to alleviate unconsciousness and casts light upon a path toward a socially-responsible way of being in the world.

Ius humanum

The following passage from Seneca offers a philosophical backdrop for a discussion of a praxis of teaching Classics for social justice:

> *possim breviter hanc illi formulam humani officii tradere: omne hoc, quod vides, quo divina atque humana conclusa sunt, unum est; membra sumus corporis magni. Natura nos cognatos edidit, cum ex isdem et in eadem gigneret. Haec nobis amorem indidit mutuum et sociabiles fecit. Illa aequum iustumque composuit; ex illius constitutione miserius est nocere quam laedi. Ex illius imperio paratae sint iuvandis manus. Ille versus et in pectore et in ore sit: Homo sum, humani nihil a me alienum puto.* (Seneca, *Epistulae Morales*, 95. 51-53)

> I propose briefly this formula for human obligations: all that you see, that which comprises the divine or human, is one; we are members of one great body. Nature has brought us forth from *the* same stock, since she bore us out of the same and into the same matter. She brought us in and created for us mutual close friends. She bound together justice and equality; in her law, it is more miserable to harm than to suffer harm. From her rule, our hands must be prepared for helping. May this verse remain in our hearts and on our lips: I am a man, I regard nothing human as strange to me.

Despite Seneca's lofty declaration that "we are members of one great body," neither he nor the Roman populace could deny the tremendous existence of inhumanity upon humanity and its impact on Roman values and activities (Bauman, 1999). The dichotomy between the values inherent in *humanitas* and the reality of Roman life could not be philosophically reconciled, and as a practical matter, Roman law tended to allow or even foster such injustice. For its part, modern society has been simultaneously horrified and fascinated by Roman slavery, gladiatorial games, forced suicides, depraved emperors, political corruption and social oppression and inequality. Perhaps it is because such inhumanity lurks not far behind in the experiences of our own time and place that American popular culture continues to explore such themes in Roman culture. At the very least, Classics does offer a perspective, using ancient material, from which to witness and reflect on injustices, both nuanced and overt, in our own culture. A discussion of Seneca's vision of all humans as one interdependent, interrelated body, sprung from the same stuff, is one place from which to initiate the dialogue in the classical classroom around social justice issues in ancient and modern societies.

So, where would the path to social justice through classical studies begin? Thanks to the legacy that established critical pedagogy and the myriad variations of social justice issues in education, many scholars, following the work of Freire, Giroux, McLaren, Kanpol, and other theorists in critical pedagogy, have offered perspectives from which a critical pedagogy of Classics for social justice might be developed. In addition, the works of Canagarajah (2005a, 2005b), Freire (2007a, 2007b), Guilherme (2002), Kubota and Austin, (2007), Osborn (2000, 2006), and Reagan (2002a, 2009a, 2010), and Reagan and Osborn (2002) have offered arguments and frameworks that are most useful in establishing a critical pedagogy of language education. Still others (Ellsworth, 1989; Gabel, 2002; Gore, 1993, 2003; Parkes, Gore, & Ellsworth, 2009; Pennycook, 2010; Simon, 1992) have provided critical questions and important caveats that require that critical pedagogical approaches and our endeavors toward social justice education be problematized, to avoid creating new totalizing discourses, paternalistic practices, or attempting a critical pedagogy that resembles an "uncritical" movement, or a watering down that amounts simply to student-based instruction (Pennycook, 2001). As Pennycook argues, "The moment we start to accept unquestioningly the work of critical pedagogy, critical literacy, critical discourse analysis, or critical language awareness, we are no longer engaged in a critical project" (p. 138). Parkes et al. (2009) offer a poststructuralist warning regarding social justice:

> Standpoint theories that define subjects by their class, race, ethnicity, or gender, are also approached cautiously by poststructural theorists, as they frequently derive from a form of essentialism that defines the subject in too rigid categories.... From a postsructuralist perspective, the concept of social justice must be problematized, rather than accepted uncritically as a universal truth or desire. (pp. 170-171)

Foucauldian analysis, which requires an examination of the roles and rules of discourse, and seeks an understanding of knowledge/power relations in terms of historicity, hermeneutics, genealogy, and narratives is useful in constructing critiques of our own formations of concepts of critical pedagogy and social justice (Parkes et al., 2009; Pennycook, 2001). Thus, we may work within a Freirean framework for inspiration in engaging in the work of a social justice pedagogy, but we may use Foucault's notion of the productive nature of power and its flipside—resistance—to maintain our balance as we avoid the pitfalls that a naïve, overly-moralized or uncritical approach might yield.

There are several components from which we may form an integrated heart of a critical pedagogy of Classics that engages social justice. Ayers, Quinn, and Stovall (2009) offer three "pillars" or principles upon which social justice education is built: (1) equity, which entails participants ensuring fairness and equal access for all, as well as redressing and restoring injustices resulting from inequity; (2) activism, in which participants in education engage fully in critical examination of conditions and contexts in which they operate and are motivated to create change through empowered agency; and (3) social literacy, a complex principle that involves cultivation of awareness of our own identities, connections to each other, and the contexts within which we function. Saltman (2009) also points out the importance of historical perspective in moving forward the goals of social justice:

> History matters for democracy because it provides a form of intellectual self-defense for public citizens at a time when truth claims are increasingly legitimized by the power of the claimant.... [P]ublic culture is increasingly subject to an eternal present and an active forgetting. This has, in part, to do with the commodification of knowledge and information as it is largely produced and circulated by corporate media with financial and ideological interests in selling fleeting spectacle for passive consumption. In fact public schooling remains one of the few places ... where knowledge and information can be investigated and debated as the basis for more complex and historically informed perspectives that can be the basis for greater individual and social understanding and public deliberation and action. (p. 2)

Galinsky (1992) argued for the relevance of Classics in lending an historical perspective on such notions as postmodernism, multiculturalism, and decline (the last of which Galinsky notes is a modern obsession, particularly evidenced in comparisons of modern American society and that of ancient Rome). As he sought to define the validity and boundaries of using the ancient world to illuminate the modern, he correctly warned that, in projecting modern issues into the past, or using the past to comprehend the contemporary, there is a danger of indulging in anachronistic correspondences between the ancient and modern worlds. This admonition is well-taken, particularly if we are to avoid universalizing or totalizing conceptualizations that obfuscate or limit the debate and which contribute to the "active forgetting" that Saltman decries.

In classical language education, whether we are examining works of literature, art, architecture, and the like, or reading funeral inscriptions and graffiti, or exploring elements of grammar or conversing in Latin, there are opportunities present for dialogue about concepts that initiate critical awareness in areas such as the nature of power and its imbalance, the content and context of what we are learning, as well as how and why, and what is missing. Therefore, to develop a critical pedagogy of Classics, one that rests upon equity, activism and social literacy, teachers may consider the tools available through which we may construct a curricular framework—

the standards, textbooks, literature, and other materials—and examine them through a critical lens. Incorporating students into the processes and contexts of instruction, curriculum and the classroom is not only important from a pedagogical standpoint, but also necessary to achieving the goals of a critical pedagogy. However, as postmodern critiques of critical pedagogy have noted (see Gore, Ellsworth, and Pennycook, cited above), we must be aware of the asymmetrical relationship between teachers and students, and the problems inherent in viewing teachers as grantors of students' "empowerment" through our pedagogical practices. As McLaren (1998), Giroux (2005) and others have pointed out, schooling is fundamentally political, never neutral, and we must be mindful of this and our own limitations when we attempt to create a democratic educational experience (or choose not to, as the case may be). So, the dynamics of the classroom environment itself function in a microsociety in which we may challenge ourselves to seek balance and acquire understandings related to equity, activism and social literacy.

Becoming aware of the agendas that exist in the social justice pedagogy, those which are teacher- and student-based, intentional and unintentional, explicit and implicit, begins with questioning and reflecting on such questions as (see Parkes et al., 2009):

- Who benefits from critical/social justice pedagogy?
- Who determines what those benefits are, and who should receive them?
- How can we know what constitutes social justice – will we "know it when we see it?" and what do we do with that knowledge?
- Are there other ways of understanding justice that are available only to those who are privileged with or by such understanding?

We can and should engage our students in these questions, and use them throughout the educational experience (during the length of a course, a year, or several years) to illuminate our practices and the intentions behind them, and to motivate action to create a more just, equitable, and activist education.

In language education, teachers must critically examine the function and purposes of what they do in the classroom, as a means of reflecting on where their practice may inhibit or nurture student learning, privilege or oppress students and their knowledge or ways of knowing, or where their practice promotes social justice or perpetuates imbalance or injustice. It is also helpful to illuminate the "metalinguistic content" that is part of the curriculum and instructional practice through questioning, as we engage students in learning languages and learning about language (Reagan &

Osborn, 2002). The following are examples of types of questions that may be used to unpack the metalinguistic aspects within our curriculum and instructional practices in language education:

- What experiences, background, or histories of language use do my students bring with them, and how are they situated within the curriculum and instruction?
- What attitudes about language do we see conveyed in the curriculum, materials and instruction we employ in the classroom?
- What is actually taught, within and outside of linguistic and cultural elements, and how is it taught?
- How is knowledge about language created, by whom is it created, and who controls it? How is language control demonstrated?
- What identities are constructed within and because of the content and context in which language teaching and learning occur in my classroom?
- How can we counteract the negative effects of constrained identities that limit student potential for access to and use of language?
- How do I as teacher use the knowledge I possess as classroom "expert" in ways that help or harm my students, and what may I do to mitigate negative effects of the knowledge imbalance between me and my students?

Again, these questions provoke teachers and students to move toward deepening their understanding of what they do, why they do it, and to recall Foucault's phrase, "what what they do does" in the context of being members of the classroom society and as students of the content. Because of the centrality of language in the human experience, and as language education and knowledge of its use is closely tied to power relations, it is incumbent upon those who adopt a critical stance to acknowledge the nature of the power (or resistance) it produces, and which produces it.

To return to the matter of developing a critical pedagogy of Classics, it may be useful to explore the component of classical studies that has been the topic of much professional discussion among classicists in recent years: Latin language pedagogy. The goal of the exploration that follows is not to "do" critical pedagogy or social justice education on the pages herein, but rather to discuss aspects of classical language teaching from a critical stance. Further, it is inappropriate and artificial (and nearly impossible, in any case) to discuss the teaching of Latin in isolation from history, culture, and other contexts in which it exists (including the classroom); therefore, these components are implicitly or explicitly contained in what follows.

Much of the discourse surrounding Latin language pedagogy in at least the past two decades has increasingly focused on improving teaching and learning of the language, increasing student's success in using Latin, and clarifying the purpose(s) of learning Latin in the first place. None of these are new concerns (in fact they have been part of lively discussion throughout the centuries), but at least some of the vigor that has characterized recent arguments was precipitated by a real or imagined crisis regarding the viability of Classics as a field (Culham & Edmunds, 1989; LaFleur, 1987, 1998). The development of *National Standards for Classical Language Learning* in 1996 provided some of the impetus for a newly-articulated vision for teaching and learning classical languages that attempted to match in form and idea that of the modern languages, so that Classics and classicists did not "take a back seat in these times of innovative reform" (Abbott, 1998, p. 37). The conversation around the teaching of Latin in the 1990s through the present has focused on a dichotomous view of methodologies employed, namely those which profess to teach Latin as a language, and those which purport to teach Latin as a puzzle to be decoded with the goal of translation (Abbott, 1998; Pearcy, 2010). According to some (Pearcy, 2010), this view emerges from discourse regarding a rift between traditional philology and its "scientific" approach (which would be aligned with the so-called grammar-translation approach—in other words, the Latin-as-puzzle methods), and the liberal, humanist, and more learner-centered/sensitive approach (the Latin-as-communicative-language). Thrown into the controversy have been developments in language acquisition theory, particularly from the field of cognitive psychology and second language acquisition (SLA) theory, the former of which influenced the development of so-called "reading method" approaches and textbooks (which presumably allow students to read large chunks of Latin very early in their experience), and the latter of which influenced methods such as total physical response (TPR) and teaching proficiency in reading through storytelling (TPRS) (Sebesta, 1998). The developments and controversies regarding Latin language teaching and learning have had a variety of effects—some dramatic, some less so—on teachers, students, and the research agenda of the profession, but one thing is clear: they are ripe for critical examination.

While it may be an overstatement that in Classics we suffer under the weight of an ontological insecurity, an image problem, or an identity crisis in our profession, it is reasonable to note that the affects of the discourse described above have prompted both a healthy curiosity about the nature of the boundaries within which teachers and students of Classics function, and a increasing tendency toward entrenchment among practitioners identifying themselves as part of one camp or another. A browse through the archives of the *Latinteach* or *CambridgeLatin* online discussion groups[8]

reveals the energy and emotion that swirls around the discussion surrounding Latin language pedagogy. Hence, we should be encouraged to
explore some of the critical questions (and those related to metalinguistic
issues) that have been listed above toward an analysis of how these views
of pedagogical practices may be problematic or problematized. First, we
may examine assumptions that may or may not reflect realities in classical
language classrooms, assumptions about the experiences, background, or
histories of language use that students bring with them. As Reagan
(2009a) and other have pointed out, in the language classroom the
teacher exists as the sole "expert," keeper of the knowledge about content, and in the practice of language education, knowledge is withheld
systematically until the teacher deems it appropriate to release bits and
pieces of awareness to correspond with what the teacher perceives as student readiness or as appropriate to the curriculum. In Latin language
pedagogy, there are distinctly different schools of thought regarding how
much, what type of, and when to release content knowledge to students.
Traditional approaches (known commonly as the grammar-translation
method) might typically release in one year nearly all of the grammar
paradigms and sometimes thousands of vocabulary words to students,
who would be responsible for memorizing all of it in order to acquire the
ability to translate authentic Latin texts during the following years of
study. Newer approaches (such as the reading method) are designed to
release grammar in bits and shorter vocabulary lists, in sequences, determined usually by textbook authors and occasionally modified by teachers
using the textbooks, that focus on use of limited grammar concepts in the
context of stories of increasing length, so that students would be able to
read Latin immediately without the burden of overwhelming amounts of
grammar in isolation. "Active" Latin approaches include considerable
amounts of spoken Latin (sometimes with a goal of *tantum Latine* in classroom talk), and involve kinesthetic learning techniques such as TPR and
TPRS. Instruction is often based on Krashen's theories of comprehensible
input/output and the importance of the affective domain in language
acquisition. Teachers release smaller bits of grammar and vocabulary to
be examined in context, with emphasis on combining aural and oral skills
in communicative practice.[9]

In each of these approaches, there is the danger that teacher- or curric-
ulum-based assumptions about student capabilities, backgrounds, desires,
and participation in the experience of language use serve to limit student
access to language learning, attach relative values to certain types of
learning or skills, and establishes "rules" for how Latin is learned (or
learnable). Regardless of the method, each one described locates the
teacher firmly at the center of the curriculum and instruction (sometimes
dominating the text, sometimes dominated by the text), with students as

vessels on the periphery, waiting to be filled. Each of the approaches has been effective for some students and teachers in the teaching and learning of Latin, but not one ensures a process for empowerment of students, which is arguably a goal for all pedagogy in a democratic society. All approaches warrant critical scrutiny by teachers and students, and with practice in critical questioning in the classroom, they may learn to recognize, question, and transform the discourse and practices that constrain and limit the formation of a just society. Latin class may appear to be a small arena in life's landscape, but it may also provide ample room for practicing a critical pedagogy.

The complexity of societies in today's world requires that students develop critical awareness that reaches across cultures. One of the tools of language pedagogy—the Five C's of the *National Standards of Foreign Language Learning* (2006) (including communication, culture, connections, comparisons, and communities—articulates some aspects of critical awareness. As was discussed previously in Chapter 4, while the Five C's may serve as an entry into opportunities for reflection, there are some ways in which the *Standards'* approach to these categories are incomplete or problematic. Further, there are additional components that are absent in the *Standards'* Five C's but which are vital elements to a social justice stance. To the Five C's we may also add these C's: critical consciousness, compassion, constructive action, and commitment to personal, professional, and collective responsibilities for the empowerment of all. The Five C's of the *Standards* represent important facets of an education in modern or classical language studies, while the additional C's suggested here refer to the aspects of a pedagogy to foster social justice that can be very appropriately applied in foreign language education, including classical education, to broaden perspectives and the scope of the impact of critical awareness. Such concepts recall domains that Guilherme (2002) posited as structures within development of a critical awareness in foreign language education, as follows:

- Interaction between self and other—in which identities are multi-layered and develop in negotiations between self and other, and which entail power relations;
- The cultural dimension—which examines narratives that are constantly being produced and reproduced with in a "web of tensions," which challenge commonsense and taken-for-granted assumptions regarding cultural identities and constructs;
- The educational dimension—in which discussions about the complexities of producing meaning should be fostered;

- The political dimension—in which it is recognized that learning and interactions cannot be depoliticized; and,
- The ethical dimension: in which the relationship between culture and power is a moral and ethical issue. (pp. 121-124)

Guilherme's (2002) model, which focused strongly on issues of cultural identity and the political nature of language education and citizenship offers a supportive layer or lens that may serve to empower the Five C's and the *National Standards* toward a deeper understanding of what is possible to think and do within a critical pedagogy of language (classical or modern) education for social justice. In each of the dimensions, teachers of Classics will find many avenues for exploring classical cultural attitudes, experiences, and artifacts (including texts) that correspond with the investigations they provoke.

Another avenue through which teachers may engage in critical curriculum and instructional practices is through what Reagan and Osborn (Osborn, 2000; Reagan & Osborn, 2002) have called "curriculum nullification," a process through which teachers choose to act in "dialogical fashion" or resistance to curriculum demands that stand in the way of social justice. Acknowledging that "teachers exercise curricular nullification every day when the classroom door closes and they begin to conduct classes in the way that they believe to be most appropriate" (Reagan & Osborn, 2002, p. 87), curriculum nullification asserts teacher (and, potentially, student) veto power as a means of recognizing the potential power inherent in their pedagogy. Reagan and Osborn describe several types of curriculum nullification, including the following: subtractive curriculum nullification, in which a teacher refuses to teach some content mandated by the curriculum; additive curriculum nullification, in which a teacher makes the decision to incorporate a content component not present in the written curriculum; and, dissonantal curriculum nullification, in which a teacher experiences "an internal check" when some aspect of the curriculum is in conflict with a teacher's beliefs. Curriculum nullification may be ethical, done with the purpose of advancing social justice, or unethical, done with the purpose or result that is equivalent to professional malpractice (pp. 87-89). Teachers of classical languages may engage in curriculum nullification when they chose to include in their teaching examples of ancient graffiti, raising critical questions related to how graffiti may be interpreted, what cultural values they represent or oppose, and how we may use them to extend our understanding of ancient cultures, particularly the segments of populations that tend to be marginalized in most Latin curricula, beyond the literary texts the curriculum requires (this would represent an additive form of curriculum nullification). Classics teachers may experience dissonantal curriculum nullification (and may potentially engage in subtractive curriculum nulli-fication) when the textbook required by the written curriculum uses ste-reotypical characters engaged in stereotypical activities or ways of behaving (such as girls who are always afraid, boys who are mischievous, mothers who are snappish, and fathers who are always busy), ostensibly as a means of appealing to young modern Latin learners, but which serve to create false or irrelevant notions about ancient society and distract from more authentic understanding of Latin culture. Teachers who engage their student in explorations of bias in curriculum and curricular materi-als, with the end of raising critical conscious and even motivating action (such as engaging students in rewriting chapters of the text to oppose such characterizations) are engaging in curriculum nullification.

In putting Classics on the path to social justice through a critical peda-gogy, we may use the following to create a vision for what teaching and learning, curriculum and praxis would look like. Therefore, a model of teaching Classics for social justice must include commitments to:

- An intention to grasp the "partiality of our understanding" (both the inherent incompleteness and bias);
- An effort to seek avenues for social justice cooperatively, with stu-dents, teachers, parents and community members, to make our understandings become progressively more complete.
- A unification among "disciplines" or content areas within Classics that transcends boundaries among concepts taught and people involved in teaching and learning, so that we understand the inter-relatedness of ways of thinking and knowing.
- A circumspect, continuous, and collaborative examination of the ways in which we are constrained by our partisanship and isms - ethnocentrism, sexism, racism, ageism etc.
- A conception of our learning as a dialogue with ourselves and the world in a self-critical way.
- A commitment to community and the exploration of tensions, dif-ference, preconceptions, and bias, so that we may take action to alleviate their affects on our community.
- An active seeking-out of materials and texts from classical origins that are outside of traditional pedagogical materials that serve to bring "words and worlds" (Freire, 1970) on the margins into focus.

γνῶθι σεαυτόν

In the development of a critical pedagogy of Classics or classical lan-guage learning, it is vital to understand how we as teachers and students function within and are limited by definitions of terminology such those contained in the Five C's, such as language, communication, culture, comparisons, connection, and community. Ambiguity and ambivalence about what these terms actually mean, and what they mean to whom, create both problems and possibilities for teachers and students engaged in the always-political processes of language learning. Osborn, Reagan, and Freiberg (2011) recently proposed a protocol for a research approach for language studies that could be used to assemble a more comprehensive view of classical language pedagogy, particularly as we endeavor to engage in a critical pedagogy. Textual concept critical analysis (TCCA), provides an analytical alternative to quantitative and various types of qualitative research that allow us to move beyond the positivism of quantitative research and the limitations of qualitative research, so that we may understand the interplay of power, texts, concepts, and context in a way that advances our understanding of what occurs in language studies. This avenue for research may help to illuminate the dark corners of our experiences of teachers and learners of Classics, as we explore the way in which classical language learning is situated within the context of foreign language learning. In particular, we would use TCCA to understand more about the problems and potential of teaching and learning Classics from a critical stance through an examination of our practices using the methodology of TCCA that Osborn et al. outline: corpus selection, thematic analysis, conceptual analysis, and trustworthiness. For example, were we to conduct an analysis of the discourse surrounding the dichotomous view of language pedagogy at the secondary level, we might choose to limit our corpus selection to reflect what we have chosen to focus on within—perhaps the most commonly used textbooks (perhaps further defining textbook series as supporting one or more of the language learning approaches described previously), or methodological texts, or online fora used by Latin teachers, or journals devoted to classical pedagogy, etc. Regarding thematic analysis, we would likely explore questions regarding the composition of the community of Classics teachers: what ages, professional experiences, geographic areas, ethnicities, genders, and so on, are represented in this community? Questions related to themes present in the goals for Latin learning that are articulated by students and teachers would also be pertinent in a thematic analysis, as would the nature of activities students and teachers engage in, such as conferences and competitions. Conceptual analysis would likely bring us into the very tricky realm of examining what language "learning" really refers to, especially when in Classics there are so many valuative assessments made about the capacity to "read," "translate," "use" Latin, "compose" Latin, etc., or to acquire "proficiency," "fluency," "mastery," and so on. For that matter, the discourse demonstrates the existence of multiple understandings or interpretations of Latin as a "language," as opposed to some other treatment of it in the teaching of students who are engaged in learning Latin. In this regard, it appears that a research methodology such as TCCA may be extremely useful for opening and expanding the conversation around the potential and problems inherent in teaching Classics, especially in adopting a critical pedagogy in Classics.

There remains much more to be considered regarding how a critical pedagogy of Classics for social justice might be constructed. Informed as we may be by our understanding of the historical backdrop of Classics in America, of the "critical" as envisioned by our midwives (Socrates, Freire, and Foucault), and by our own critiques of practices, principles and proposals, the more questions should and in fact do surface. With each question that surfaces, we may continously find that, like Socrates, we are wisest because, above all, we know nothing. In the security of that knowledge, we are compelled, then, to move forward.

NOTES

1. Greco-Roman relationships were among the most complex in antiquity, and much classical scholarship has been engaged in study of the interplay of Greek language and culture and Roman power. See Adams (2003), Gruen (2011), and Whitmarsh (2010).

2. See Richard A. Bauman's (1999) discussion of the nature of *humanitas* as it related to notions of human rights in Ancient Rome. Bauman describes the multifaceted understanding of *humanitas*, conveyed most clearly by Cicero and Seneca, as a congregation of other traditional Roman values, such as *clementia, liberalitas, virtus,* and the ancient Greek ideal of φιλανθρωπία (*philanthropia*). He also reminds us that, for the Romans (as in ancient Greek and even contemporary American society), power still determines how, to whom, by whom and under what circumstances *humanitas* was conveyed: "Elitism, always entrenched in Roman society, was considered perfectly compatible with *humanitas*" (p. 71).

3. Liddel (2007) and Herman (2006) assert a continuity between civic obligations and personal liberties as a characteristic of Athenian democracy that worked successfully; however, Matthew Christ (2006) disagrees with both, arguing that Athenian citizens struggled with their obligations and were not as noble about fulfilling those responsibilities (such as military service) as they have been romanticized to have been, citing Aristotle in this regard: "all men, or most men, wish what is noble but choose what is profitable" (*Nicomachean Ethics,* 1163a1).

4. An interesting example to consider is the reception and interpretations of Plato's *Republic* throughout the centuries. As Annas (2000) points out, in contrast with the way in which *Republic* has been viewed in the twentieth and twenty-first centuries (i.e., as one of the primary works in the canon of

philosophy, and the most widely read, with Plato as one of the most important philosophers in history) in ancient times, *Republic* was not considered the centerpiece of Greek philosophy, nor was it regarded even as one of Plato's most important works. The themes and ideas it contained did not enter the mainstream of political thought in ancient Greece the way that some of Plato's other dialogues had. *Republic* was studied in the medieval era by the Islamic tradition in the East as guidance for religious leadership, but was ignored in the Christian West. While it attracted some attention by humanists in the Renaissance, it was not until the late nineteen century, when the famed classicist Benjamin Jowett (who translated all of Plato into English and made his works accessible to the public) placed *Republic* at the core of classical curriculum (p. 29), where it acquired long-lived regard as a source for inspiring debate on contemporary issues of the nineteenth and twentieth centuries such as democracy, the just state, the ideal leader, and the intersection of politics and philosophy.

5. For example, the first century C.E. Roman philosopher Seneca, as well as philosophers and scholars of the Middle Ages, Renaissance and Enlightenment referred to and adapted Cicero's idea of *humanitas* (Gay, 1995; Kristeller, 1955).

6. Hogan uses the term "partiality" to refer both to incompleteness and to bias that limits understanding.

7. See Plato's *Apology* 21d.

8. See Latinteach at latinteach@nxport.com ; also CambridgeLatin at CambridgeLatin@yahoogroups.com .

9. Pennycook (2001) is extremely critical of SLA work, due to its emphasis on the cognitive processes of language learning that ignore or distort the ways in which social, cultural or political realities affect the context of learning. Because SLA has "operated with a positivistic research methodology, … it has tended to view learning environments and learners as settings in which 'variables' need to be controlled" (p. 142).

APPENDIX

For readers who are not fully comfortable with phrases in Latin and Greek, the following are provided as an additional assistance. It should be noted that I have deliberately chosen to use specific Latin and Greek phrases, most of which come from literature, in the text; however, in many instances the translations—no matter how accurate they may be—do not do full justice to the linguistic and cultural meanings of the original. The translations are provided by page number:

Page	Latin/Greek	English Translation
Dissertation Title	*Consilio et Animis*	by wisdom and heart
Chapter 1 Title	*Consilium*	Purpose
1	*exilium tempus barbariumque locum*	in a time of exile and a barbaric place
4	*Longa tibi exilium*	a long exile for you
6	*Decipimur specie recti*	We are deceived by the appearance of the right
9	*Quo usque tandem abutere?*	Up to what point will (you) abuse us?
Chapter 2 Title	*Auctoritas*	Authority
22	*Ab initio*	From the beginning
23	*mos maiores*	the ways of the ancestors
27	*Imperium sine fine*	Empire without end
32	*Multa quoque et bello passus*	*having suffered much in war*
37	*Ad nostra tempora*	to our own time

(Appendix continues on next page)

Latin and Greek Translations Continued

Page	Latin/Greek	English Translation
38	*anima sana in corpore sano*	healthy mind in healthy body
Chapter 3 Title	*Veritas*	Truth
48	*Forsan et haec olim meminisse iuvabit*	Perhaps one day it will delight to remember even this
55	*Audentis Fortuna iuvat*	Fortune aids the bold
61	*Ne credite equo*	Don't believe the horse
Chapter 4 Title	*Civitas*	Citizenship
76	*Summum ius summa iniuria*	The more law, the more harm
79	τῷ δ' ἐνὶ θυμῷ θῆκε μένος καὶ θάρσος	In his heart she placed strength and courage
82	*Unde venis?*	Whence do you come?
85	*Et tu?*	You too? Even you?
87	*Cui bono?*	For whose benefit?
Chapter 5 Title	*Humanitas*	Philanthropy, erudition, learning
103	*Ius humanum*	Law governing human relations
112	γνῶθι σεαυτόν	Know yourself

REFERENCES

Abbott, M. G. (1998). Trends in language education: Latin in the mainstream. In R. Lafleur (Ed.), *Latin for the 21st century: From concept to classroom* (pp. 36-43). Glenview, IL: Addison-Wesley.

Adams, H. (1918). *The education of Henry Adams: An autobiography.* Boston, MA: Houghton Mifflin.

Adams, J. N. (2003). *Bilingualism and the Latin language.* Cambridge, England: Cambridge University Press.

Álvarez, I. (2007). Foreign language education at the crossroads: Whose model of competence? *Language, Culture and Curriculum, 20*(2), 126-139.

American Classical League. (1997). *Standards for classical language learning.* Oxford, OH: Miami University.

Annas, J. (2000). *Ancient philosophy: A very short introduction.* New York, NY: Oxford University Press.

Apple, M. W. (1995). *Education and power.* New York, NY: Routledge.

Apple, M. W. (2001). *Educating the "Right" way: Markets, standards, God, and inequality.* London: RoutledgeFalmer.

Apple, M. W. (2004). *Ideology and curriculum.* New York, NY: Routledge.

Apple, M. W., Au, W., & Gandin, L. A. (Eds.). (2009a). *The Routledge international handbook of critical education.* New York, NY: Routledge.

Apple, M. W., Au, W., & Gandin, L. A. (2009b). Mapping critical education. In In *The Routledge international handbook of critical education* (pp. 3-19). New York, NY: Routledge.

Apple, M. W., & Beane, J. A. (2007). *Democratic schools: Lessons in powerful education* (2nd ed.). Portsmouth, NH: Heinemann.

Arendt, H. (1977). *Between past and future: Eight exercises in political thought.* New York, NY: Penguin.

Ayers, W., Quinn, T., & Stovall, D. (Eds.). (2009). *Handbook of social justice in education.* New York, NY: Routledge.

120 **A. M. RYAN**

Ball, S. (1990). *Foucault and education: Disciplines and knowledge*. London: Routledge.

Ball, S. (2001). Performativities and fabrications in the education economy: Towards the performative society. In D. Gleeson & C. Husbands (Eds.), *The performing school: Managing, teaching, and learning in a performance culture* (pp. 210-226). London: RoutledgeFalmer.

Ball, S. J. (2003). The teacher's soul and the terrors of performativity. *Journal of Education Policy, 18*(2), 215-228.

Bauman, R. A. (1999). *Human rights in ancient Rome*. London: Routledge.

Beard, M., & Henderson, J. (2000). *Classics: A very short introduction*. Oxford, England: Oxford University Press.

Bennett, W. J. (1993). *The book of virtues*. New York, NY: Simon & Schuster.

Berliner, D. C., & Biddle, B. J. (1995). *The manufactured crisis: Myth, fraud and attack on America's public schools*. New York, NY: Addison-Wesley.

Beyer, L. E., & Apple, M. W. (Eds.). (1998). *The curriculum: Problems, politics and possibilities* (2nd ed.). Albany, NY: State University of New York Press.

Blackledge, A. (2000). *Literacy, power and social justice*. Stoke on Trent, Staffordshire, England: Trentham.

Bracey, G. W. (2004). *Setting the record straight: Responses to misconceptions about public education in the U.S.* (2nd ed.). Portsmouth, NH: Heinemann.

Bracey, G. W. (2006). *Reading educational research: How to avoid getting statistically snookered*. Portsmouth, NH: Heinemann.

Campbell, D. T. (1979). Assessing the impact of planned social change. *Evaluation and Program Planning, 2*(1), 67-90.

Canagarajah, A. S. (2005a). Reconstructing local knowledge, reconfiguring language studies. In A. S. Canagaraja (Ed.), *Reclaiming the local in language policy and practice* (pp. 3-23). Mahway, NJ.: Lawrence Erlbaum.

Canagarajah, A. S. (2005b). Critical pedagogy in L2 learning and teaching. In E. Hinkel (Ed.), *Handbook of research in second language teaching and learning* (pp. 931-950). Mahway, NJ: Lawrence Erlbaum.

Carson, P. P. (1993) Deming versus traditional management theorists on goal setting: Can both be right? *Business Horizons*. Retrieved from http://findarticles.com/p/articles/mi_m1038/is_n5_v36/ai_14723299/pg_8/?tag=content;col1.

Cartledge, P. (1998). Classics: From discipline in crisis to (multi-) cultural capital. In Y. L. Too & N. Livingstone (Eds.), *Pedagogy and power: Rhetorics of classical learning* (pp. 16-28). Cambridge, England: Cambridge University Press.

Case, B. J. (2005, September). *The age of accountability*. Summary of Keynote Address, from the 2005 China–U.S. conference on Aligning Assessment With Instruction, Beijing, People's Republic of China. San Antonio, TX: Pearson. Retrieved from http://www.pearsonassessments.com/NR/rdonlyres/9B951F2F-37A6-4508-A656-3EF8FE346B19/0/AgeofAccountability.pdf

Chomsky, N., & Macedo, D. (2000). *Chomsky on miseducation*. Lanham, MD: Rowman & Littlefield.

Christ, M. A. (2006). *The bad citizen in classical Athens*. Cambridge, England: Cambridge University Press.

Counts, G. S. (1932). Dare progressive education be progressive? *Progressive Education*, *9*(4), 257-263.

Counts, G. S. (2004). Dare the school build a new social order? In D. J. Flinders & S. J. Thornton (Eds.), *The curriculum studies reader* (pp. 25-30). New York, NY: RoutledgeFalmer.

Culham, P., & Edmunds, L. (Eds.). (1989). *Classics: A discipline and profession in crisis?* Lanham, MD: University Press of America.

Darder, A. (2003). Teaching as an act of love: Reflections on Paulo Freire and his contributions to our lives and our work. In A. Darder, M. Baltodano, & R. Torres (Eds.), *The critical pedagogy reader* (pp. 497-510). New York, NY: RoutledgeFalmer.

Darder, A., Baltodano, M., & Torres, R. (Eds.). (2003). *The critical pedagogy reader*. New York, NY: RoutledgeFalmer.

Dearden, R. F., Hirst, P. H., & Peters, R. S. (1972). *Education and the development of reason*. London: Routledge & Kegan Paul.

De Lissovoy, N. (2008). *Power, crisis, and education for liberation: Rethinking critical pedagogy*. New York, NY: Palgrave Macmillan.

Deming, W. E. (2000) *Out of the crisis*. Cambridge, MA: MIT Press.

Demont-Heinrich, C. (2008). American "prestige press" representations of the global hegemony of English. *World Englishes*, *27*(2), 161-180.

Dewey, J. (2004). *Democracy and education*. Mineola, NY: Dover.

Dillon, S. (2010, December 3). Teacher ratings get new look, pushed by a rich watcher. *The New York Times*, p. A1.

Dreyfus, H. L., & Rabinow, P. (1983). *Michel Foucault: Beyond structuralism and hermeneutics*. Chicago, IL: University of Chicago Press.

Drucker, P. (1993). *The practice of management*. New York, NY: HarperCollins.

duBois, P. (2001). *Trojan horses: Saving the Classics from the conservatives*. New York, NY: New York University Press.

Du Bois, W. E. B. (1961). *The souls of Black folk*. Raleigh, NC: Hayes Barton Press.

Du Bois, W. E .B. (2005). *Darkwater: Voices from within the veil*. Retrieved from Project Gutenberg website: http://www.gutenberg.org/etext/15210

Elgin, S. H. (2000). *The language imperative: The power of language to enrich your life and expand your mind*. New York, NY: Perseus.

Edwards, J. (2010). *Language and identity: An introduction*. New York, NY: Cambridge University Press.

Ellsworth, E. (1989). Why doesn't this feel empowering? Working through the repressive myths of critical pedagogy. *Harvard Educational Review, 53*(9), 297-324.

Evans, R. W. (2007). *This happened in America: Harold Rugg and the censure of social studies*. Charlotte, NC: Information Age.

Farrell, J. (2001). *Latin language and culture*. Cambridge, England: Cambridge University Press.

Foucault, M. (1969). *L'archéologie du savoir* [The archaeology of knowledge]. Paris, France: Éditions Gallimard.

Foucault, M. (1972). *The archaeology of knowledge and The discourse on language* (A. M. Sheridan Smith, Trans.). New York, NY: Pantheon. (Original work published 1969).

Foucault, M. (1975). *Surveiller et punir* [To Discipline and to punish]. Paris: Éditions Gallimard.

Foucault, M (1980). *Power/knowledge: Selected interviews and other writings*. New York, NY: Pantheon Books.

Foucault, M. (1988). Technologies of the self. In L. H. Martin, H. Gutman, & P. H. Hutton (Eds.), *Technologies of the self: A seminar with Michel Foucault* (pp. 16-49). Amherst, MA: University of Massachusetts Press.

Foucault, M. (2000). *Power. Essential works of Michel Foucault* (J. Faubion, Ed.). (R. Hurley, Trans.). New York, NY: New Press.

Foucault, M. (2001) *Fearless speech*. Los Angeles: Semiotext(e).

Foucault, M. (2003). *The birth of the clinic: An archeology of medical perception*. (A.M. Sheriden, Trans.) London: Routledge. (Original work published 1963).

Foucault, M. (2006). *History of madness*. (J. Murphy & J. Khalfa, Trans.). London: Routledge. (Original work published 1961).

Foucault, M. (2007). *The politics of truth*. Los Angeles, CA: Semiotext(e).

Freire, P. (1970). *Pedagogia do oprimido* [Pedagogy of the oppressed]. Rio de Janiero: Paz e Terra.

Freire, P. (1994). *Pedagogy of hope: Reliving Pedagogy of the oppressed*. New York, NY: Continuum.

Freire, P. (1996). *Pedagogia da autonomia: Saberes necessários à prática educativa* [Pedagogy of autonomy: Knowledge necessary for educational practice]. São Paulo, Brazil: Paz e Terra.

Freire, P. (2001). *Pedagogy of freedom: Ethics, democracy, and civic courage* (P. Clarke, Trans.). Lanham, MD: Rowman & Littlefield.

Freire, P. (2007a). *Daring to dream: Toward a pedagogy of the unfinished* (A. K. Oliveira, Trans.). Boulder, CO: Paradigm.

Freire, P. (2007b). *Education for critical consciousness*. New York, NY: Continuum.

Friedman, T. L. (2006). *The world is flat: A brief history of the twenty-first century*. New York, NY: Farrar, Straus and Giroux.

Fronsdal, G. (2005). *The Dhammapada: A new translation of the Buddhist classic, with annotations*. Boston, MA: Shambhala.

Gabel, S. (2002). Some conceptual problems with critical pedagogy. *Curriculum Inquiry, 32*(2), 177-207.

Galinsky, K. (1992). *Classical and modern interactions: Postmodern architecture, multiculturalism, decline, and other issues*. Austin, TX: University of Texas Press.

Gaisser, J. H. (2002). The reception of classical texts in the Renaissance. In A.J. Grieco, M. Rocke, & F. Giofreddi Superbi (Eds.), *The Italian Renaissance in the twentieth century* (pp. 387-400). Florence, Italy: The Harvard University Center for Italian Renaissance Studies.

Galinsky, K. (1998). *Augustan culture*. Princeton, NJ: Princeton University Press.

Gardner, D. P. (Ed.). (1983). *A nation at risk: The imperative for educational reform*. Washington, DC: U.S. Department of Education.

Gay, P. (1995). *The Enlightenment: The rise of modern Paganism*. New York, NY: W. W. Norton.

Giroux, H. A. (1988). *Teachers as intellectuals*. Westport, CT: Bergin & Garvey.

Giroux, H. A. (2003a). Critical theory and educational practice. In A. Darder, M. Baltodano, & R. Torres (Eds.), *The critical pedagogy reader* (pp. 27-55). New York, NY: Taylor & Francis.

Giroux, H. A. (2003b). Public pedagogy and the politics of resistance. *Educational Philosophy and Theory, 35*(1), 5-16.

Giroux, H. A. (2005). *Schooling and the struggle for public life: Democracy's promise and education's challenge*. Boulder, CO: Paradigm.

Glass, G. V. (2008). *Fertilizers, pills and magnetic strips: The fate of public education in America*. Charlotte, NC: Information Age.

Glass, R. D. (2001). On Freire's philosophy of praxis and the foundations of liberation education. *Educational Researcher, 30*(2), 15-25.

Goulah, J. (2010). Dialogic resistance in education. In D. M. Moss & T. A. Osborn (Eds.), *Critical essays on resistance in education* (pp. 83-104). New York, NY: Peter Lang.

Gore, J. (1993). *The struggle for pedagogies: Critical and feminist discourses as regimes of truth*. London: Routledge, Chapman and Hall.

Gore, J. (2003). What we can do for you! What can "we" do for "you?" Struggling over empowerment in critical and feminist pedagogy. In A. Darder, M. Baltodano, & R. Torres (Eds.), *The critical pedagogy reader* (pp. 331-350). New York, NY: RoutledgeFalmer.

Gramsci, A., & Buttigieg, J. (2002, Summer). From the "Prison Notebooks." *Daedalus, 131*(3), 71-83.

Gruen, E. (2011). *Rethinking the other in antiquity*. Princeton, NY: Princeton University Press.

Guilherme, M. (2002). *Critical citizens for an intercultural world: Foreign language education as cultural politics*. Clevedon, England: Multicultural Matters.

Gutek, G. L. (2006). George S. Counts and the origins of Social Reconstruction. In K. L. Riley (Ed.). *Social reconstruction: People, politics, perspectives* (pp. 1-26). Charlotte, NC: Information Age.

Hankins, J. (1990). *Plato in the Italian Renaissance* (Vol. 1). New York, NY: E. J. Brill.

Hanson, V. D., & Heath, J. (1998). *Who killed Homer?: The demise of classical education and the recovery of Greek wisdom*. New York, NY: Free Press.

Hart, G. L. (2000). *Statement on the Status of Tamil as a classical language*. Retrieved from http://tamil.berkeley.edu/tamil-chair/letter-on-tamil-as-a-classical-language.

Held, D. (1980). *Introduction to critical theory: Horkheimer to Habermas*. Berkeley, CA: University of California Press.

Herman, D. (2007). It's a small world after all: From stereotypes to invented worlds in secondary school Spanish textbooks. *Critical Inquiry in Language Studies: An International Journal, 4*(2-3), 117-150.

Herman, G. (2006). *Morality and behavior in democratic Athens: A social history*. New York, NY: Cambridge University Press.

Hill, B. (n.d.) *Latin for students with learning disabilities* [Brochure]. Northfield, MN: Classical Association of the Midwest and South.

Hirst, P. H. (2010). Liberal education and the nature of knowledge. In R. D. Archambault (Ed.), *Philosophical analysis and education* (pp. 76-95). London: Routledge & Kegan Paul.

Hirst, P. H., & Peters, R. S. (1970). *The logic of education*. London: Routledge & Kegan Paul.

Hogan, P. (1998, August). *Paideia, prejudice, and the promise of the practical*. Paper presented at the 29th World Congress of Philosophy, Boston, Massachusetts.

Hoskin, K. (1990). Foucault under examination: The crypto-educationalist unmasked. In S. Ball (Ed.). *Foucault and education. Disciplines and knowledge* (pp. 29-55). London: Routledge.

Hurlburt, T. (1869). *Transactions of the American Philological Association, 1(1869-70)*, 5-30.

Hymes, D.H. (1996). *Ethnography, linguistics, narrative inequality: Toward an understanding of voice*. London: Taylor & Francis.

Jaeger, W. (1986). *Paideia: The ideals of Greek culture, Volume 1: Archaic Greece: The mind of Athens* (2nd ed.). Oxford, England: Oxford University Press.

Janson, T. (2004). *A natural history of Latin*. Oxford, England: Oxford University Press.

Jay, M. (1996). *The dialectical imagination: A history of the Frankfurt School and the Institute of Social Research, 1923-1950*. Berkeley, CA: University of California Press.

Jones, M., & Vickers, D. (2011, March). *Considerations for performance scoring when designing and developing next generation assessments*. Retrieved from http://www.pearsonassessments.com/hai/images/tmrs/Performance_Scoring_for_Next_Gen_Assessments.pdf

Kanpol, B. (1993, March). An educational challenge: Working through a philosophical contradiction. *Clearing House, 66*(4), 241.

Kanpol, B. (1998). *Critical pedagogy for beginning teachers: The movement from despair to hope*. Retrieved August 4, 2008, from Monash University: http://users.monash.edu.au/~dzyngier/Critical%20Pedagogy%20For%20Beginning%20Teachers%20Barry%20Kanpol.htm

Kanpol, B. (1999). *Critical pedagogy: An introduction* (2nd ed.). Westport, CT: Greenwood.

Kincheloe, J. L. (2008). *Critical pedagogy primer*. New York, NY: Peter Lang.

Kopff, E. C. (2000). *The Devil knows Latin: Why America needs the classical tradition*. Wilmington, DE: Intercollegiate Studies Institute.

Kramsch, C. (2000). Second language acquisition, applied linguistics and the teaching of foreign languages. *The Modern Language Journal, 84*(3), 311-326.

Krashen, S. D., & Terrell, T. D. (1983). *The natural approach: Language acquisition in the classroom*. London: Prentice Hall Europe.

Kristeller, P. O. (1955). *The Classics and Renaissance thought*. Cambridge, England: Harvard University Press.

Kronman, A. T. (2007). *Education's end: Why our colleges and universities have given up on the meaning of life*. New Haven, CT: Yale University Press.

Kubota, R. (2004). The politics of cultural difference in Second Language Education. *Critical Inquiry in Language Studies, 1*(1), 21-39

Kubota, R., & Austin, T. (2007). Critical approaches to world language instruction in the United States: An introduction. *Critical Inquiry in Language Studies, 42*(2-3), 73-83.

LaFleur, R. A. (Ed.). (1987). *The teaching of Latin in American schools: A profession in crisis.* Chico, CA: Scholars Press.

LaFleur, R. A. (Ed.). (1998). *Latin for the 21st century: From concept to classroom.* Glenview, IL: Addison-Wesley.

Lamb, S. A. (1994). *Official English and the foreign language teaching profession: A survey of attitudes.* (Unpublished doctoral dissertation, University of Delaware). Retrieved from Dissertations & Theses: Full Text. (Publication No. AAT 9516338).

Lather, P. (1998). Critical pedagogy and its complicities: A praxis of stuck places. *Educational Theory, 48*(4), 487-497.

Lather, P. (2001). Ten years later, yet again: Critical pedagogy and its complicities. In K. Weiler (Ed.), *Feminist engagements: Reading, resisting and revisioning male theorists in education and cultural studies* (pp. 183-195). London: Routledge.

Lee, V. E., & Ready, D. D. (2009). U.S. high school curriculum: Three phases of contemporary research and reform. *The Future of Children, 19*(1), 135-156.

Leonardo, Z. (2004). Critical social theory and transformative knowledge: The functions of criticism in quality education. *Educational Researcher, 33*(6), 11-18.

Liddell, P. (2007). *Civic obligation and individual liberty in ancient Athens.* Oxford, England: Oxford University Press.

Lin, A. (2004). Introducing a critical pedagogical curriculum: A feminist reflexive account. In B. Norton & K. Toohey (Eds.), *Critical pedagogies and language learning* (pp. 271-290). New York, NY: Cambridge University Press.

Liu, Y. (2005). Discourse, cultural knowledge and ideology: A critical analysis of Chinese language textbooks. *Pedagogy, Culture & Society, 13*(2), 233-264.

Luke, A. (2004). Two takes on the critical. In B. Norton & K. Toohey (Eds.), *Critical pedagogies and language learning* (pp. 21-29). New York, NY: Cambridge University Press.

Luke, C., & Gore, J. (1992). *Feminisms and critical pedagogy.* New York, NY: Routledge.

MacKay, S. L., & Wong, S. C. (1988). Language teaching in nativist times: A need for sociopolitical awareness. *The Modern Language Journal, 72*(4), 379-388.

Martin, J. R. (2002). *Cultural miseducation: In search of a democratic solution.* New York, NY: Teachers College Press.

Manzo, K. (2006, March 29). Students taking Spanish, French; Leaders pushing Chinese, Arabic. *Education Week, 25*(29), 1, 25.

McLaren, P. (1998). Revolutionary pedagogy in post-revolutionary times: Rethinking the political economy of critical education. *Educational Theory, 48*(4), 431-463.

McLaren, P. (1999). A pedagogy of possibility: Reflecting upon Paulo Freire's Politics of Education: In Memory of Paulo Freire. *Educational Researcher, 28*(2), 49-56.

McLaren, P. (2003). Critical pedagogy: A look at the major concepts. In A. Darder, M. Baltodano, & R. Torres (Eds.), *The critical pedagogy reader* (pp. 27-55). New York, NY: RoutledgeFalmer.

Meckler, M. (Ed.). (2006). *Classical antiquity and the politics of America*. Waco, TX: Baylor University Press.

Meier, D. (2000). *Will standards save public education?* Boston, MA: Beacon.

Meier, D. (2007, May). *Campbell's Law and testing* [Blog post]. Retrieved from http://blogs.edweek.org/edweek/Bridging-Differences/2007/05/campbells_law_and_testing.html

Mount, H. (2007). *Carpe diem: Put a little Latin in your life*. New York, NY: Hyperion

Mount, H. (2007, December). A vote for Latin. *The New York Times*. Retrieved from http://www.nytimes.com/2007/12/03/opinion/03mount.html

Mulcahy, D. G. (2008). *The educated person: Toward a new paradigm for liberal education*. Lanham, MD: Rowman & Littlefield.

National Governors Association Center for Best Practices and Council of Chief State School Officers. (2010). *Common core state standards initiative*. Washington, DC: Author.

National Institute of Child Health and Human Development. (2000). *Report of the National Reading Panel. Teaching children to read: an evidence-based assessment of the scientific research literature on reading and its implications for reading instruction: Reports of the subgroups* (NIH Publication No. 00-4754). Washington, DC: U.S. Government Printing Office.

National Standards in Foreign Language Education Collaborative Project. (1996). *The standards for foreign language learning in the 21st century)*. Lawrence, KS: Allen Press.

National Standards in Foreign Language Education Collaborative Project. (1999). *Standards for foreign language learning: Preparing for the 21st century* (2nd ed.). Lawrence, KS: Allen Press.

National Standards in Foreign Language Education Collaborative Project. (2006). *The standards for foreign language learning in the 21st century* (3rd ed.). Lawrence, KS: Allen Press

Neuman, J. (2008). A poem in other words is a language lesson. *Classical Journal, 104*(1), 67-71.

Nichols, S. L., & Berliner, D. C. (2007). *Collateral damage: How high-stakes testing corrupts America's schools*. Cambridge, MA: Harvard Education Press.

Nieto, S. (1999). *The light in their eyes: Creating multi-cultural learning communities*. New York, NY: Teachers College Press.

Noddings, N. (2005). *The challenge to care in schools: An alternative approach to education* (2nd ed.). New York, NY: Teachers College Press.

Mathis, W. J. (2010). *The "Common Core" Standards Initiative: An effective reform tool?* Boulder and Tempe: Education and the Public Interest Center & Education Policy Research Unit. Retrieved from http://epicpolicy.org/publication/common-core-standards.

Office of the Press Secretary. (2011, January 25). Remarks by the President in State of Union Address. Washington, DC: The White House. Retrieved from http://www.whitehouse.gov/the-press-office/2011/01/25/remarks-president-state-union-address.

Olssen, M. (1996). In defence of the welfare state and publicly provided education: A New Zealand perspective. *Journal of Education Policy, 11*(3), 337-362

Ortega, L. (1999). Rethinking foreign language education: Politics of the profession. In K. A. Davis (Ed.), *Foreign language teaching and language minority education.* (pp. 21-39). Honolulu, Hawai'i: University of Hawai'i Press.

Osborn, T. A. (2000). *Critical reflection and the foreign language classroom.* Westport, CT: Greenwood Publishing Group.

Osborn, T. A. (2006). *Teaching world languages for social justice: A sourcebook of principles and practices.* Mahway, NJ: Lawrence Erlbaum Associates.

Osborn, T. A., Reagan, T. G., & Freiberg, J. (2011). Textual concept critical analysis: Toward a research approach for language studies. *Critical Inquiry in Language Studies, 8*(1), 1-26.

Oxford, R. (2010). Second language education: With liberty and languages for all. In T. K. Chapman & N. Hobbel (Eds.), *Social justice pedagogy across the curriculum: The practice of freedom* (pp. 299-308). New York, NY: Routledge.

Parkes, R. J., Gore, J. M., & Ellsworth, W. (2010). After Poststructuralism: Rethinking the discourse of social justice pedagogy. In T. K. Chapman & N. Hobbel (Eds.), *Social justice pedagogy across the curriculum: The practice of freedom* (pp .164-183). New York, NY: Routledge.

Partnership for 21st Century Skills (2009). P21 Frameworks Document. Retrieved from http://www.p21.org/ index.php?option=com_content&task=view&id=254&Itemid=119

Pavlenko, A. (2003). "Language of the enemy:" Foreign language education and national identity. *International Journal of Bilingual Education and Bilingualism, 6*(5), 313-331.

Pearcy, L. T. (2005). *The grammar of our civility: Classical education in America.* Waco, TX: Baylor University Press.

Pearcy, L. T. (2010, Spring). Preparing classicists or humanists? *Teaching Classical Languages, 1*(2), 192-195. Retrieved from http://tcl.camws.org/ spring2010.html

Pearson (2011). Pearson Provides Recommendations for Performance Scoring of Next Generation Student Assessments [Press Release]. Retrieved from http:// www.pearsonassessments.com/pai/ai/about/news/NewsItem/ newsrelease032311b.htm.

Pennycook, A. (2001). *Critical applied linguistics: A critical introduction.* Mahwah, NJ: Lawrence Erlbaum Associates.

Pennycook, A. (2004a). Critical moments in a TESOL practicum. In B. Norton & K. Toohey (Eds.), *Critical pedagogies and language learning* (pp. 327-345). New York, NY: Cambridge University Press.

Pennycook, A. (2004b). Performativity and language studies. *Critical Inquiry in Language Studies: An International Journal, 1*(1), 1-19.

Ponder, G. (2006). Social reconstructionist curriculum impulses: Pragmatism, collectivism, and "the American Problem." In K. L. Riley (Ed.), *Social reconstruction: People, politics, perspectives* (pp. 235-255). Charlotte, NC: Information Age Publishing.

Popham, W. J. (2004). Standards-based education: Two wrongs don't make a right. In S. Mathieson & E. W. Ross (Eds.), *Defending public schools: The nature and limits of standards-based reform and assessment* (Vol. IV., pp. 15-29). Westport, CT: Greenwood.

Popkewitz, T., & *Brennan*, M. (1998). *Foucault's challenge: Discourse, knowledge and power in education*. New York, NY: Teachers College Press.

Ransom, R. L. (1993). *Conflict and compromise: The political economy of slavery, emancipation, and the American Civil War*. Cambridge, England: Cambridge University Press.

Ravitch, D. (1995). *National standards in American education: A citizen's guide*. Washington, DC: The Brookings Institution.

Ravitch, D. (2010). *The death and life of the great American school system: How testing and choice are undermining education*. New York, NY: Basic Books.

Reagan, T. (2002a). *Language, education, and ideology: Mapping the linguistic landscape of U.S. schools*. Westport, CT: Praeger.

Reagan, T. (2002b). Toward an "archeology of deafness": Etic and emic constructions of identity in conflict. *Journal of Language, Identity and Education, 1*(1), 41-66.

Reagan, T. (2004). Objectification, positivism and language studies: A reconsideration. *Critical Inquiry in Language Studies: An International Journal, 1*(1), 41-60.

Reagan, T. G. (2009a). *Language matters: Reflections on educational linguistics*. Charlotte, NC: Information Age.

Reagan, T. (2009b, November). *Sine qua non? Liberal education, the "educated person," and foreign language study*. Paper presented at the meeting of the American Educational Studies Association, Pittsburgh, PA.

Reagan, T. (2010). Critical pedagogy in the foreign language education context: Teaching Esperanto as a subversive activity. In D. M. Moss & T. A. Osborn (Eds.), *Critical essays on resistance in education* (pp. 47-66). New York, NY: Peter Lang.

Reagan, T. G., & Osborn, T. A. (2002). *The foreign language educator in society: Toward a critical pedagogy*. Mahway, NJ: Lawrence Erlbaum Associates.

Reese, W. J. (2005). *America's public schools: From the common school to No Child Left Behind*. Baltimore, MD: Johns Hopkins University Press.

Rhodes, N. H., & Pufahl, I. (2009). *Foreign language teaching in U.S. schools: Results of a national survey*. Washington, DC: Center for Applied Linguistics.

Richard, C. (1994). *The Founders and the classics: Greece, Rome, and the American Enlightenment*. Cambridge, MA: Harvard University Press.

Richard, C. (2009). *The golden age of the classics in America: Greece, Rome, and the antebellum United States*. Cambridge, MA: Harvard University Press.

Riley, K.L. (2006). *Social reconstruction: People, politics, perspectives*. Charlotte, NC: Information Age.

Robertson, N. (2006). Platonism in high places: Leo Strauss, George W. Bush and the response to 911. In M. Meckler (Ed.), *Classical antiquity and the politics of America* (pp. 153-174). Waco, TX: Baylor University Press.

Rothstein, J. (2011, Jan. 13). Review of *Learning about teaching: Initial findings from the measures of effective teaching project* by Bill and Melinda Gates Foundation. Boulder, CO: National Education Policy Center. Retrieved from http://nepc.colorado.edu/thinktank/review-learning-about-teaching.

Rothstein, R. (1998). *The way we were? The myths and realities of America's student achievement*. New York, NY: The Century Foundation Press.

Rugg, H. O. (1921). Reconstructing the curriculum: An open letter to Professor Henry Johnson commenting on committee procedure as illustrated in the report of the Joint Committee on History and Education for Citizenship. In W. Parker (Ed.), *Educating the democratic mind* (pp. 45-60). Albany, NY: State University of New York Press.

Ruiz, R. (1988). Orientations in language planning. In S. L. MacKay & S. L. Wong (Eds.), *Language diversity: Problem or resource? A social and educational perspective on language minorities in the United States* (pp. 3-25). New York, NY: Newbury House.

Saltman, K. J. (2009). Historical and theoretical perspectives. In W. Ayers, T. Quinn, & D. Stovall (Eds.), *Handbook of social justice in education* (pp. 1-3). New York, NY: Routledge.

Sebesta, J. L. (1998). *Aliquid semper novi:* New challenges, new approaches. In R. LaFleur (Ed.), *Latin for the 21st century: From concept to classroom* (pp. 15-24). Glenview, IL: Addison-Wesley.

Sehlaoui, A. (2008). Language learning in the United States of America. *Language, Culture & Curriculum, 21*(3), 195-200.

Sercu, L. (2000). *Acquiring intercultural communicative competence from textbooks: The case of Flemish adolescent students learning German.* Leuven, Belgium: Leuven University Press.

Shardakova, M., & Pavlenko, A. (2004). Identity options in Russian textbooks. *Journal of Language, Identity & Education, 3*(1), 25-46.

Shields, J. C. (2001). *The American Aeneas: Classical origins of the American self.* Knoxville, TN: University of Tennessee Press.

Shor, I. (1992). *Empowering education: Critical teaching for social change.* Chicago, IL: University of Chicago Press.

Shor, I., & Freire, P. (2003). What are the fears and risks of transformation? In A. Darder, M. Baltodano & R. Torres (Eds.), *The critical pedagogy reader* (pp. 27-55). New York, NY: Taylor and Francis.

Shorey, P. (1919). Fifty years of classical studies in America. *Transactions and Proceedings of the American Philological Association, 50,* 33-61.

Simon, R. (1992). *Teaching against the grain: Essays towards a pedagogy of possibility.* London: Bergin & Garvey.

Sizer, T. (1996). *Horace's Hope: What works for the American high school.* New York, NY: Houghton Mifflin.

Sleeter, C. E., & Grant, C. A. (2007). *Making choices for multicultural education: Five approaches to race, class, and gender* (6th ed.). Hoboken, NJ: Wiley.

Slouka, M. (2009, September). Dehumanized: When math and science rule the school. *Harper's Magazine, 319,* 32-40.

Smith, W., Wayte, W. & Marindin, G. E. (Eds.) (1890). *A dictionary of Greek and Roman antiquities* (3rd ed.). London: John Murray.

Teitelbaum, K. N. (1998). Contestation and curriculum: The efforts of American Socialists, 1900-1920. In L. E. Beyer & M. W. Apple (Eds.), *The curriculum: Problems, politics and possibilities* (2nd ed., pp. 34-57). Albany, NY: State University of New York Press.

Tocqueville, A. (1904). *Democracy in America* (Henry Reeve, Trans.). New York, NY: D. Appleton.

Too, Y. L., & Livingstone, N. (Eds.). (1998). *Pedagogy and power: Rhetorics of classical learning*. Cambridge, England: Cambridge University Press.

Tozer, S. E., Violas, P. C. & Senese, G. (2002). *School and society* (4th ed.). New York, NY: McGraw Hill.

Trumbull, J. H. (1869). *Transactions of the American Philological Association (1869-96), 1*(1869-70), 5-30.

U.S. Department of Education, Office of Postsecondary Education. (2008). Enhancing Foreign Language Proficiency in the United States: Preliminary Results of the National Security Language Initiative, Washington, DC. Retrieved from http://www.ed.gov/about/inits/ed/competitiveness/nsli/about.html

Vinovskis, M. (1998). *History and educational policy making*. New Haven, CT: Yale University Press.

Watkins, W. (2006). Social reconstruction in education: Searching out Black voices. In K.L. Riley (Ed.). *Social reconstruction: People, politics, perspectives* (pp. 211-235). Charlotte, NC: Information Age.

Wallace-Hadrill, A. (2008). *Rome's cultural revolution*. Cambridge, England: Cambridge University Press.

Waquet, F. (2001). *Latin, or, the empire of the sign: From the sixteenth to the twentieth century*. London: Verso.

Watzke, J. L. (2003). *Lasting change in foreign language education: A historical case for change in national policy*. Westport, CT: Praeger.

Vistaviista, T. (Ed.). (2010). *Local knowledge and microidentities in the imperial Greek world*. New York, NY: Cambridge University Press.

Widmer, T. (2008). *The ark of the liberties*. New York, NY: Hill and Wang.

Wink, J. (2005). *Critical pedagogy: Notes from the real world* (3rd ed.). Boston, MA: Pearson.

Winterer, C. (2002). *The culture of Classicism: Ancient Greece and Rome in American intellectual life*. Baltimore, MD: Johns Hopkins University Press.

Winterer, C. (2006). Classical oratory and fears of demagoguery in the antebellum era. In M. Meckler (Ed.), *Classical antiquity and the politics of America* (pp. 41-54). Waco, TX: Baylor University Press.

Worth, F. (1993, Fall). Postmodern pedagogy in the multi-cultural classroom: For inappropriate teachers and imperfect spectators. *Cultural Critique, 25*, 5-32.

Yale Report of 1828. (1828). *Part II: A report on the liberal course of education*. Retrieved from http://collegiateway.org/reading/yale-report-1828/curriculum

Yong, Z. (2007, September). Can we meet the demand? *Phi Delta Kappan*, p. 42. Retrieved from Academic Search Premier database.

Ziobro, W. J. (2006). Classical education in colonial America. In M. Meckler (Ed.), *Classical antiquity and the politics of America* (pp. 13-28). Waco, TX: Baylor University Press.